Please Sit Over

How to Manage **Power,**
Overcome **Exclusion,**
and **Succeed** as a
Black Woman at Work

There

FRANCINE PARHAM

BK

Berrett–Koehler Publishers, Inc.

Berrett-Koehler Publishers, Inc.
1333 Broadway, Suite 1000
Oakland, CA 94612-1921
Tel: (510) 817-2277
Fax: (510) 817-2278
www.bkconnection.com

ORDERING INFORMATION

Quantity sales. Special discounts are available on quantity purchases by corporations, associations, and others. For details, contact the "Special Sales Department" at the Berrett-Koehler address above.

Individual sales. Berrett-Koehler publications are available through most bookstores. They can also be ordered directly from Berrett-Koehler: Tel: (800) 929-2929; Fax: (802) 864-7626; www.bkconnection.com.

Orders for college textbook / course adoption use. Please contact Berrett-Koehler: Tel: (800) 929-2929; Fax: (802) 864-7626.

Distributed to the U.S. trade and internationally by Penguin Random House Publisher Services.

Berrett-Koehler and the BK logo are registered trademarks of Berrett-Koehler Publishers, Inc.

Printed in the Canada

Berrett-Koehler books are printed on long-lasting acid-free paper. When it is available, we choose paper that has been manufactured by environmentally responsible processes. These may include using trees grown in sustainable forests, incorporating recycled paper, minimizing chlorine in bleaching, or recycling the energy produced at the paper mill.

Library of Congress Cataloging-in-Publication Data
Names: Parham, Francine, author.
Title: Please sit over there : how to manage power, overcome exclusion, and
     succeed as a Black woman at work / by Francine Parham.
Description: First edition. | Oakland, CA : Berrett-Koehler Publishers,
     2022. | Includes index.
Identifiers: LCCN 2022002429 (print) | LCCN 2022002430 (ebook) | ISBN
     9781523001521 (paperback ; alk. paper) | ISBN 9781523001538 (pdf) | ISBN
     9781523001545 (epub)
Subjects: LCSH: African American women executives. | Women executives. |
     Career development. | Discrimination in employment. | Sex discrimination
     in employment.
Classification: LCC HD6054.4.U6 P367 2022 (print) | LCC HD6054.4.U6
     (ebook) | DDC 658.4/092082--dc23/eng/20220317
LC record available at https://lccn.loc.gov/2022002429
LC ebook record available at https://lccn.loc.gov/2022002430

First Edition

30 29 28 27 26 25 24 23 22   10 9 8 7 6 5 4 3 2 1

Book production: Seventeenth Street Studios

Cover design: Nita Ybarra

Illustration by Jeni Paltiel / Lellobird

*To my Mother, Juanita, and my Father, Oscar Sr.,
who taught and told me all that they knew.*

CONTENTS

My Message to Black Professional Women

"I'm not telling you what I heard; I'm telling you what I know." This was one of my father's favorite sayings. He said this to me when I was a child and later when I was an adult. It has served me as a creed throughout my adult life and career, and it is the place from which I speak as I write these words. It is what I know that I want to pass on to the Black women building their careers and lives today.

In two decades as a Black woman in the institution of corporate America, I have learned a lot, I have witnessed a lot, and I have experienced a lot. I have made many decisions and was a part of many more, and eventually I reached the highest levels of leadership. I have been at *the table*.

My road wasn't easy, nor was my path defined. I don't take for granted the many amazing and strong-willed Black women who made a path for me. Even though many of these women were not from the corporate sector, they stood up for me. And when they stood up for what they believed in, they afforded me the privilege of being able to sit down in those rooms at those leadership tables.

Their advocacy left me with a responsibility to bring more Black women to positions of leadership and authority in the workplace. It is my life's work to bring more of us to the table, not just as tokens or symbols but in roles with genuine authority and influence. We have a long way to go in this journey despite the fact that we are neither new nor inexperienced within these many institutions.

I am not satisfied with what should accurately be called a lack of progress. We are still not at the tables and in the rooms where we need to be, especially in the institutions of corporate America. But Black women in the workplace are at an inflection point. I have heard many advocates say that they want to help us but they aren't quite sure how to get us there. Out of this dissatisfaction, I offer a way forward. An important lesson I have learned in corporate America is to never complain without a recommendation and ultimately, a solution.

My solution is to talk about the concept of power. Power is not bad; it is the people behind it and their actions that have the potential to make it corrupt or evil in nature. My goal is to help black women understand power and learn how to use it to their own benefit, accelerating their career trajectory and professional advancement. It is unfortunate when the concept of power carries negative connotations. In the context I am considering in this book, power leveraged for your career advancement is a good thing. I believe that learning this skill is the key to bringing more Black women to that proverbial table. And you do have power—everyone does, even in the workplace. It's how you use it and what you use it for that matters.

One thing I'd like to note: you won't ever hear me talk about Black women becoming empowered. We already have that covered. We have been empowered for a very long time. Self-efficacy is not something that I have a problem with, nor have I seen my sisters struggle with self-efficacy. I was raised to know that I am powerful. I have my mother, my role model, and my father to thank for that.

I have come to understand what power means, who has it, and the importance of using it to help me succeed in the workplace. My intention is to share what I know in the hope that it will help you create or enhance your own career by understanding what your organization values, what you value, and how you can get to a position of power.

I also see embracing power as a part of your economic advancement and the economic advancement of all Black women. The equation is simple: the higher you go in an organization, the more money you should make (or should at least be asking for). This is what will allow you to have the life you choose for yourself or others. These are the stakes you are playing for.

I'm not the first to talk about career advancement, and I hope not to be the last voice to talk about this specifically with regard to Black women, but I am a Black professional woman who has discovered what it takes to rise to power at work. My journey has been long and rich. I have been given this privilege. I do not take it for granted, and I feel that I have a responsibility to use my voice. We are playing by a set of rules that we never agreed to and that we were never trained for. I want to share with Black women how they too can succeed.

Here's what I know to be true: once we have a workplace that works for Black women, we can have a workplace that works for all. That has not happened yet. I can't change what has happened in the past, but I can impact what is happening today and in the future. I am choosing to share all that I know and to use the power of my experience and my voice to help you.

I encourage you to share and discuss this book not only with people in your network but also within your organization and with your leader. Create a dialogue to let the organization know what your expectations are and how they can help you. This book is not for you alone. With this book I intend to help you create change in your organization for yourself and for others—to join me in carrying it forward. I'll for sure continue to do my part.

I was so excited I could hardly contain myself. I took one last look around and opened the screen door to exit my home, carrying the last set of items to an old car that was to carry me from Joppatowne, Maryland, to West Lafayette, Indiana, where I would become a freshman at Purdue University.

I was beaming with delight, as any 17-year-old would be, about to embark on an amazing journey. I was ready to leave all that I knew and take on something new. And most exciting, I would be away from the watchful eye of my parents, especially my father and his extremely high expectations. I couldn't get out the front door fast enough! I finally felt that I was free—or so I thought.

"Squirt," I heard my father say, using the nickname he had called me since birth. I paused in midstep when I heard his voice. He was sitting in a chair by the front door and appeared to be looking in my direction but he wasn't looking at me, which was odd. He'd always told his children to look directly at him when he was speaking to us. He'd witnessed too many years of Black people bowing their heads when they were spoken to. But this time, my father was not about to tell another story or wish me well. I could tell by the lack of eye contact that he was about to share something of deep personal significance. He appeared to be deep in his own thoughts, recalling something I will never know.

Roots

I grew up in a home where race and the disparities that my parents had experienced were a topic of everyday conversation. Discussing and dissecting world events concerning Black folk was a part of our everyday lives.

My mother was an activist in her younger years. She walked the picket lines in the 1960s as a college student and later became an educator. She even carried phone numbers for specific journalists at the *Washington Post* so she could tell them what she was seeing in her community of Lynchburg, Virginia.

My father's family grew up picking cotton in Emporia, Virginia. His father was a sharecropper, and my father also became an educator. Both parents ensured that all six of their children took formal education seriously. They also told us about their lives as Black people. The stories of their lived experiences conveyed lessons and sage advice that guided me both as I was growing up and as I navigated corporate America. What I learned then still guides me today.

In that moment, my father didn't look at me and I didn't look at him. He said, "Make sure that you watch and pay attention. You represent thousands of us." I'm sure this sounds familiar if you are Black. I stopped, looked at the ground, and said only, "OK, Daddy." In that moment, I knew what he meant, but as a 17-year-old, my understanding was largely theoretical. As I moved through my life, I would come to have a much deeper and more nuanced understanding of what he meant.

This line transcends generations in the Black community. I heard it as I was growing up and I continue to hear it today from people who are parents. I'm sure many of you have heard this as well. Although we, as Black people, preach the virtues of individuality and being measured on our own merit, we know that we are often still judged collectively based on the actions of even just a single one of us. Truly, what my father told me then still has meaning today.

My father was not telling me simply to watch what I said or to remember that my words and actions would impact how white people perceived my race as a whole. No, what he was saying was much deeper. He was also telling me to be mindful of what I said, how I said it, when I said it, why I was saying it, and, most important, who I said it to.

You may say, "Francine, that was a lot of interpretation from one sentence." And I would say to you, "Yes, yes it was."

But my mother and father had trained me to listen. I don't ever remember a time when we weren't talking about what was happening in the world. We analyzed the world's events by considering what was said and who said it and what our own critical perspective was. Our parents would ask my siblings and me if we thought someone's voice had been heard or what it was we thought someone wanted to achieve. Were they working on behalf of moving humanity forward (or not)—and was that lofty goal even possible? What was our opinion? What were our thoughts? What would we do differently?

My father's words and everything I learned from my family ultimately took me to the very pinnacle of corporate America, where I have held positions as a global executive and a vice-president in Fortune 500 companies. And now I have a goal of helping Black professional women in the workplace. I hope that the experiences that led to my successes, what I learned from my failures, and how I succeeded in spite of missteps will help others advance in their careers.

The Goal and How to Get There

Black women want to be successful. We want to have amazing careers. We want to be in positions of leadership and authority in our workplaces. And we are already qualified to do so. There is no shortage of ambitious Black women in the professional talent pipeline, despite the tired, erroneous narrative that we can't be found.

Navigating professional institutions to achieve career advancement and success is especially challenging when many of us are battling other issues that mire us down and distract us from our goals. There is nothing empowering about working for an institution where you must perform your best but must also overcome bias, discriminatory institutional practices, and exclusion, all the while seeing that privileges that many folks take for granted often do not include you.

I've lived through this and I have watched other Black professional women experience this, as I'm sure many of you who are reading this book have. Even if you are not a Black woman, you can understand that this is our reality.

I learned one thing during my career that mattered most and that became the key to my success. It's something we often overlook or are misinformed about. The term itself often carries a negative connotation, but career advancement and success requires that we leverage it to our advantage.

What I am referring to is power. This book is about the concept of power. Specifically, this book is about helping Black professional women at all career levels understand and learn how power works and how it can serve as a strategy for career success and advancement.

As I navigated corporate America as a leader and global executive for two decades, I saw how understanding power is critical to professional advancement. I learned what power was, how it operated within organizations, and most importantly who had it. I share my stories to provide you with an understanding how to make power work for you. Know that the title of "leader" does not always denote power. Power is made up of unspoken skills and invisible rules that were not written by Black women or for Black women. But it is associated with rules that Black women need to master if they are to succeed in the corporate world.

What You Say and Who You Say It To

As I navigated corporate America years after my father's comment to me, I came to realize that he had been teaching me about being strategic about my messages and how I presented them. I learned that I had to listen and watch with the intention of responding appropriately. Ultimately, this is how I learned what it means to control my narrative. My narrative became a powerful tool as I gained progressively more senior roles in the companies where I worked.

The tone you use is as important as the narrative you tell. I learned that when my father told me to listen, he wasn't just talking about messages but also about the tone with which those messages were delivered. Knowing *how* to deliver the message is just as important as the information you are delivering.

After knowing what your message is and how to deliver it, knowing who to deliver the message to is the final key to leveraging your power. As you have probably already observed, power is not always where you think it is. Those who seem to have it may not always be the ones who actually have it. To navigate the conduits of power in an organization, you must learn to identify the true sources of influence, no matter where they show up. When your goal is career advancement, building and nurturing relationships strategically is a crucial skill.

I could never have found my power in corporate America without the sage advice my parents instilled in me to watch and listen. You must know and understand the environment you are in in order to respond to it. This is how you get the results you want in any goal you set in your professional life. Your success and career advancement as a Black woman in the workplace will be no different.

This book will help you understand how to be deliberate about forming the relationships you will need to succeed in your career. It will help you build and maintain those relationships by showing you how to use your voice strategically.

A quick housekeeping note: I've told many stories from my own career in this book and I've endeavored to maintain the anonymity of the other people in those stories. In service of that aim, names, sometimes gender, and even minor details of the stories have been changed to protect the privacy of others.

President John F. Kennedy once quoted the famous saying that "a rising tide lifts all boats." I agree with this idea 100 percent.

My only caveat is that this works only if everyone actually has a boat. My intention in this book is to ensure that everyone—and especially every Black woman—has one of those boats. I hope that sharing my experiences and what I've learned will help you manage your own career so you will be competitively positioned when the rising tide comes your way.

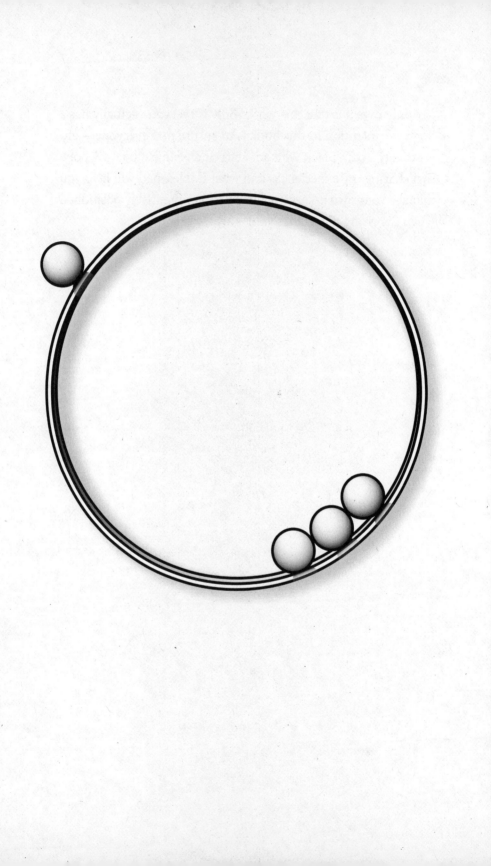

PART ONE

Where Power Comes From, Really

CHAPTER ONE

Please
Sit
Over
There

The night before my first day as the newest global vice-president of a Fortune 100 company, I drove to the building where I would be working. I wanted to make sure that I wouldn't get lost or be late. I had planned everything down to the last detail for my big debut with the organization. An announcement had been shared with every employee of the company. I had received congratulatory messages from places I didn't even know had offices in countries throughout the world. I was overwhelmed but excited.

I drove for four hours from my home straight to my new office location. I arrived at 2:00 a.m., parked, jumped out of my car, and stood in the parking lot looking at the huge building. My only thought was, "Francine, look at what you have achieved!" I hadn't screwed up. I had made it through undergraduate and graduate school and had managed to climb the ranks in two companies as a vice-president, as an executive—a title that so many Black women like me did not have but so many deserved. I still couldn't quite believe it.

The next morning, when I returned to my new office location, I was ready. But all of my excitement and feelings of pride in my accomplishment were to be short lived.

I had decided to wear a boiled-wool dress suit that day, an understated, textured fabric in a deep crimson. I wanted to be balanced but noticed for this appearance, so while I chose only a watch and basic earrings for accessories, I wore an amazing pair of red suede platform heels that matched so well you might have thought that I had bought the shoes and had had the suit made to match. In fact, I had. I was dressed to reflect the statement I wanted to make on my first day—bold but tasteful, in a way that made me feel all the confidence of the senior leader that I was.

The words that I would use to introduce myself to my staff and executive colleagues in my first leadership meeting were etched in my brain. I parked my car, went through the front doors, and walked up to a receptionist to introduce myself. Before I could finish saying my last name, I heard a voice interrupting me, saying the words "Please sit over there."

It wasn't a request, it was a command. The receptionist didn't even look directly at me. She simply acknowledged me and pointed to a row of chairs by the wall. "You're early and the training for the associate employees hasn't started yet. Please just sit over there until we are ready," she said, emphasizing her instruction.

In that moment, I was reminded of who I was and where I *didn't* belong. I had just been minimized and relegated, presumed to be something that I was not. Something that I had worked so hard to achieve felt as if it had just disappeared and didn't matter anymore.

"Did I just hear what I thought I heard?" I thought to myself.

What happened to me demonstrated what my parents had told me about and what every Black person in America knows to watch out for—being stereotyped. This was not the first time I'd experienced the misuse of power by others that so many of us as Black women in the workplace experience in our careers. We are often told to wait our turn. We receive feedback that we're not quite ready or that we are super smart but not smart enough that those in power feel comfortable taking a risk on us. (I found that particularly interesting; as if we wouldn't be smart enough to figure it out!)

All of my work and experience in corporate America had brought me to this critical moment in my career as a leader. I had trained and had practiced controlling my reactions in situations worse than this one. I had learned through watching others over the years that choosing my reactions strategically rather than reactively was the key to being the one in control—the one with the power.

Make no mistake that when she spoke those words to me, giving me a command, she was in charge. The hierarchy was flipped. I was many organizational levels above her. The key was that I knew this and I had an opportunity to choose my response. I could have used my voice and tone to put her in her place, letting her know who I was to take back my power. If only it were that simple.

I was being directed to move myself out of the way while others moved freely through the lobby. She had relationships with them, not me, and she was unquestionably in control. She was the gatekeeper. And despite her lower level in the organizational chart, I knew immediately that she could make my entrance into my new executive role much harder. I was aware that I could correct her misunderstanding, but she possessed relationships that I did not. If I reacted according to my (absolutely justified) feelings of indignation, I would spend a lot of time working to undo the damage she could do to my reputation, perhaps without even realizing what she was doing. At this point in my new job, the organization and its leaders trusted her more than they did me because they simply did not know me yet.

Maintaining control of my voice and managing my expression was the key to my power. I had no relationship with this woman at all. I didn't know who she reported to or whether she was an assistant to an executive or a temp. What I did know was that she was there for a reason and that someone had given her the authority to do what she did to me. Clearly, I didn't need to sit down, much less sit where I had been told to sit. I had no intention of doing that. But how I chose to respond to her was the power that I had. This was about getting what I wanted: a successful start in an organization where no one looked like me.

I have always wondered if the same assumption would have been made about me if I had been a white female or male. My guess is probably not. This was one of the most pointed and memorable moments where I was told what to do and the concept of power manifested itself distinctly in my thinking. The way I thought about power in that moment guided all my future actions as a professional Black woman in the workplace.

Power Is More Than an Org Chart

You might think that power follows the structure of a hierarchy, that each level at an organization conveys more power as you ascend. That is definitely not the case.

Anyone who has been an administrative assistant or has worked with an administrative assistant knows that they are the gatekeepers of the calendar. They make the decisions about who will get time on their manager's calendar and who just keeps getting pushed forward until they get the message and stop asking. They decide whether your request will be heard or not. They are often the trusted confidant of their manager and often what they say goes.

The kind of power held by an administrative assistant is a form of informal power. They may not be high in the hierarchy, but they do have the ability to control certain aspects of their organization's functioning. Make no mistake, "informal" does not mean "less." Administrative assistants may wield considerable power by virtue of their relationships with powerful people in the company. I would argue that there is even an aspect of formal power to their roles, since their authority is granted to them by someone in a position of leadership and authority.

The official organizational chart only tells you who reports to whom officially. You can assume that there is more to the network of power relationships behind the hierarchy and reporting structure on that chart. And even at the level of vice-presidents and CEOs, the real power networks may have some nuance. It's often the unofficial organizational chart that reveals the truth of who works to get things done and for whom.

How You Use Your Voice Impacts How Much Power You Have

When I was told to "please sit over there," I had a choice about how to respond. How I responded was going to have an outsized impact on the power I would wield in this new position.

I recovered quickly and thanked the receptionist for sharing that information and for pointing me in the right direction.
And then I said that my new role was reporting to the president
of the organization as the new executive vice-president. The
receptionist of course became deeply embarrassed. I smiled,
tilted my head ever so slightly, and let her apologize profusely.
I never forgot her.

Thank God for the fact that I learned to have a "clutch," as
I call it, between my brain and my mouth. I couldn't respond
like I really wanted to because thousands of Black people were
counting on me. It would have been so easy to become angry,
to raise my voice or demonstrate that I was in charge or felt
insulted. However, I knew that that would not have gone over
well. The only thing it would have gotten me would have been
a story circulating throughout the company about how the new
leader was demanding or insulting or whatever I could have been
painted to be as an outsider—a Black female outsider.

The story would have taken a life of its own and would have
been recounted or remembered in some way that would not
have been beneficial to my professional success. I purposefully
chose not to take that path. I chose not to let her have that
power over me. More important, I chose not to let the organization or any other individual have that type of power over
me. The ability to recognize these truths and predict the down-
stream impacts came from the years I'd already spent learning
the game of power in corporate America.

Like it or not, there is a game to be played. You can choose
to play it by figuring out what the game is in your organization and how you can navigate it for your own success. There
is no five-step approach to building your power. It comes over
time and it must be what works for you. But you have to be

comfortable with your voice and how you express it, regardless of what you see others doing.

But also know that you will be held accountable for what you choose to do. My key message is that *you must know what you are doing.* Your problems will begin when you don't realize that there is a game being played or when you try to pretend that there isn't one. That is when you will have given up your power unconsciously. But if you are aware of your power, you will never lose it, even if you are not the one in control at that moment. The name of the game is to get back your control.

Breaking It Down

Even though we exchanged just a few sentences, the way I chose to respond to the receptionist was highly strategic. I want to break down the component parts to show you the rational and invisible architecture behind my choices. While I made these choices in a split second, I had spent a decade in corporate America, watching, listening, and practicing, and I had plenty of missteps and learning opportunities behind me.

How I chose to respond is known as false respect or false politics. In this case, what that meant was maintaining a pleasant physical and verbal demeanor and choosing words that did not imply any adversarial intent. This of course did not reflect what I was experiencing internally. But I knew that the choice I made would place me in charge in the long run. I knew what I was doing. In that moment I had to be purposeful and strategic.

First, I thanked her for telling me to "please sit over there." Obviously, I was not genuinely thanking her, but it follows the scripted social expectation of this sort of interaction; a thank-you is polite. I did not want to make her feel defensive. I wanted her to feel comfortable in the interaction so that my next comment could have a powerful impact.

Next, it was after making her feel comfortable, but getting her full attention, that I revealed who I was. I did this without any fanfare or extensive explanation and as though it were a normal, everyday conversation. I could have been asking where the restrooms were, but I was actually letting her know that I was one of the new, most powerful leaders in her office.

And then I used the most powerful tool at my disposal: silence. I stopped speaking and simply waited for her to respond, even though the silence went on for a few moments. My silence made space for her to process what she'd just heard and for her to feel embarrassed. Silence can be impactful and it can speak as loudly as your words.

I also made a decision to use nonverbal power cues. They are often more impactful than anything else. My condescending smile, my direct look, and the tilting of my head spoke volumes. Actions speak louder than words, and I chose to use the power of actions. How many times have we watched our leaders and dissected their moves, what they have said, who they have said it to, and what happened? How many conversations have we had with our peers about this?

My goal has always been to be perceived as a leader, no matter what level I was at in my career. I always leaned into portraying the job and the role I wanted before I officially gained the leadership title or salary that went with it. Hence, once I got to this moment, I was prepared. And in this situation, it was for real. I was a leader, so I had to set the tone as a leader. People always watch how others respond, especially in a work setting. You always have the opportunity to set the tone for how you are perceived. I may have been told to "please sit over there," but I controlled my narrative and the narrative about the situation.

Power Doesn't Come from Where You Think It Does

"Make yourself invaluable" to those at work is a saying I've always lived by. As I built my career and worked more with people at the executive level, this advice came to have more importance. Even just a few years into working a corporate job, I no longer believed that my success had anything to do with my skills and abilities. Skills and the ability to perform well are a basic requirement, and I had always demonstrated them flawlessly. Career advancement is about much more than performance. But if your value doesn't come from your performance, the issue becomes how to make yourself invaluable.

I knew that all was not fair in the workplace. I had seen white males and females succeed much faster with less work experience than me and with less education or knowledge than I had. Clearly, something unseen was happening. Even if all things were equal between me and whoever I was competing with, my white colleagues often got the developmental opportunity, the visible projects, or the promotion I wanted. It surely wasn't about hard work. Showing the organization that you make money for them wasn't it either. We've all made a lot of money for our organizations, either directly or indirectly. I learned that career advancement was always situational, depending on the individuals involved, what was at stake, or who liked what you were doing. Many times it came down to who liked you in the organization.

As I became more senior in my roles over the years, I observed that others were succeeding by using unexpected and sometimes counterintuitive methods. Their power plays were often invisible, or nearly so, and didn't follow the surface-level, obvious pathways. I also realized that there were no rules or standards to guide me. The higher I climbed in my career, the more opaque the rules and standards became, to the point that they were virtually invisible to those who were not privileged enough to know them or have access to effective guidance.

I had no relationship with the woman who told me to "please sit over there." That was the critical factor that influenced who had the power in that situation. If she had known my role, she would have known to have a more appropriate interaction with me. But the absence of a relationship resulted in her power play. The question for me became, as it hopefully will for you, how I should choose to use my voice, my power, to control the narrative about me. Even though I didn't have a relationship with her, I had the opportunity to set the tone, thus protecting my ability to form the relationships I was going to need to be successful in that role.

Relationships, it turns out, are everything. Navigating power is really navigating *relationships*. It is about knowing which relationships you need, what they need to look like, how to build them, and how to leverage them for your own success and the success of others. And you build and nurture these relationships by using your voice.

Building the right strategic relationships to achieve what the organization and its leadership deemed important became the most powerful tool in my arsenal. I consciously decided to build the most strategically advantageous relationships by using the power of my voice appropriately to achieve my goal of advancing as a Black woman in corporate America.

Years of applying these lessons had led me to that lobby and that executive role. I had learned that having sponsorship, building organizational advocacy for yourself, and having a leadership story were essential. These were all things that no one told me about and that were often used to exclude me as a Black professional. Using my voice and building the right relationships had prepared me to know how to respond to that administrative assistant. My response served me well; she later became one of my advocates in the organization. Never discount anyone at first glance; you never know who they are or who they could be.

CHAPTER TWO

What You
Need
to Know
about
Power

S o what is power really? The concept of power is not new.
We see it all the time at work and it reveals itself in almost
everything that happens there. According to *Merriam-Webster
Dictionary*, power is "possession of control, authority, or influence over others." Simply stated, it is the ability to influence others. Building power through relationships is also not just about
nepotism or old-boy networks. Anyone can build, nurture,
and maintain the right relationships. In being about influenc-
ing others, power is inextricable from the relationships within
which it occurs. The right relationships can be built, nurtured,
and maintained by anyone, and your voice is the tool that you
can use to accomplish this.

We often overlook the positive value of power. In the work
environment, power is often positioned as a negative, as when
someone has too much power, resulting in a negative outcome.

It might not feel natural to think about power as a resource to help us achieve success in our careers or as something we can use to our advantage in a positive way.

Power can become invaluable if you understand what it is, who to use it with, when to use it, where you should use it, and how to use it. It can be an asset in your current role and it can also position you for professional advancement.

I discovered that as a Black professional woman navigating the corporate sector, I had the ability to influence others and that power was directly correlated with my professional success. I learned that in order to gain the degree of influence that would enable me to achieve my professional goals, I needed to make sure that I built the most strategically advantageous relationships.

When I had that insight, I also realized that my power wasn't just about me. Leveraging my power to position someone else for success was not only the right thing to do, it was a necessary part of the process. If I didn't help others grow their power, I would never be able to grow my own power. Power is about being able to use your influence on behalf of others.

The concept of power is very fluid in today's work environment. For example, it can be rooted in the context of where you are working or it can be determined by who you happen to be working with. It exists throughout an organization, even at the lowest levels in your company. I experienced this when I was told to "sit over there" by someone several levels below me but who exerted legitimate power. I was told what to do because of the position she held within the organization coupled with the specific task she had been given to manage: directing the incoming new associates. Everyone in your organization has some level of power through their relationships, including your company's executives, managers, and supervisors and those who report to them. All of these people have power, and it is important that you recognize that you do as well.

Seeing the Unseen When You're the Only One to See

The first step in learning how to navigate power is to learn how to see it. Because power is so often invisible, I fell back on the advice my father gave me to watch and listen. This helped me better understand what types of power existed in the organizations I worked for. It helped me determine who held positions of formal and informal power and recognize power when I saw it in action.

When someone enters corporate America, they are typically told "YOU own your career!" When I was told this, I understood it conceptually, but I didn't understand what I was supposed to do. Very few, if any individuals could tell me what that meant, and as a Black professional woman, there weren't a lot of people who looked like me in the organizations I worked for, so I had no role models. The saying "you have to see it to be it" didn't work for me because there was nothing for me to see.

The reality is that anyone who tells someone that they fully own their career is lying. It is even more of a falsehood when it is said to Black women. I discovered this because I began to see that all things being equal (my performance, my skills, my education, and so forth—the things I "owned" and had control over), I should have received just as many promotions and leadership opportunities as others did. However, that wasn't the case. I knew that to truly own my career, other people in the organizations I worked for and even the organizations themselves had to also share accountability for my progress.

In theory, as I climbed the corporate ranks, obtaining more senior- and executive-level positions, my own power grew. However, the higher I climbed, the less likely it was that I could find someone to watch who resembled me. My colleagues were predominantly white men.

The absence of other women and in particular other women of color, much less Black women, as role models meant that I watched the white men who were in positions of power. This enabled me to see how power worked and who had it. Every day I saw it played out by individuals who didn't look like me and didn't share my values or perspectives. At times the only benefit of being the only Black woman in my workplace was that I had a front-row seat to the power game. I saw how those in power navigated the workplace. I came to call them "the players."

When I realized that having the power to own my career was about mastering this game by using my ability to influence others to help me achieve my goals, this work became my top priority. I already had the skills to do my job successfully. My performance record was always strong, and this allowed me to focus on mastering the power game.

The Game Explained

If you're not told how to own your career and you never learn how to position yourself to be professionally successful, you will remain powerless. Institutions and those who run them have the power to keep you that way. And when this happens, it is an abuse of power. But you can overcome this by taking the time to understand the power game, learn the power of your voice, and focus on what types of power exist and how it can be used.

What I discovered was that there were no absolute rules or protocols in this game. Every situation was dependent on the context and on the players themselves. So how do you play a game that has no rules? The answer is simple: you watch the players.

From my front-row seat, I was able to observe leaders in action and learn how the power of influence worked. This experience provided me with the access and the information that I lacked, which helped me learn to play. I knew that I needed to become adept at leveraging my own power if I wanted to take my career to the heights I was aiming for.

The players are the people who have any degree of control over the organization or its individual functions. They can be executives, managers, or they might be your peers, the colleagues who work with you on projects or team members from different groups across the organization. Watch for people who seem to consistently get things done. Who is always getting their proposals approved? Which people's support always seems to be critical to making change, even when they are not the most senior players? What departments consistently get the most resources?

Identify the people who have the ability to influence others and watch what they do. This could even be the executive assistant who controls the calendar for a more obviously powerful person. It could even be the promising intern the senior leadership seems willing to listen to, despite the intern's inexperience.

Unwritten Rules

A part of playing the power game was ensuring that I was able to demonstrate often hidden but extremely important implicit skills and understand the opaque rules of the organizations I worked in. I learned that people in power (both official and unofficial) were measuring my aptitude with these unspoken skills and unwritten rules as I navigated my career. My ability to perform the tasks in my job description only got me admitted to the game. Being successful in the hidden aspects of career advancement was what really mattered.

I learned that how people assessed me and my ability to advance was based on things that weren't in my job description, such as having a solid professional story and a sound professional brand that aligned with the organization's brand, ensuring advocacy for myself within the organization as a whole, the right organizational network, and the right sponsor. These things were in addition to being able to use my power not only help myself but also to help others be successful. Obviously, these skills were not required as a part of my performance and did not show up in any of my development plans, but they were critical to achieving my career goal of becoming an executive.

No one taught me any of these implicit skills or discussed any of the opaque rules that existed in the companies I worked for. There was no training course where I could learn these things. I learned from watching, listening, and being willing to ask questions. When I realized that someone was viewed as having a strong brand or was strongly supported within the organization, I would approach them and ask them how they got to where they were. I asked them how they gained the support of what a colleague used to call "bigger players than me."

I knew that I needed people to speak on my behalf when I wasn't present and that they needed to be people the organization would believe. I discovered that I couldn't leave it up to one person to speak positively about my career goals and aspirations; I needed several people. I came to understand that I had to figure out who it was that held the power to get things done, despite what the organizational chart said. Also I had to get this task done without offending or overlooking a key player. That skill is called organizational navigation. I also figured out that it was important to have a group of individuals in my organization who could give me advice (a personal "board of directors") and that it was equally important to have a group that could actually take action on my behalf if needed. The members of this group would be on the lookout for me, protect me when I was vulnerable, and provide guardrails that would keep me in line with my organization's expectations.

I needed this group to be made up of both players within my organization and players at other organizations. Being connected only to people in my organization was not the best strategy. You never know when you may have to leave your organization or when your organization may decide to leave you. You need to be prepared and protected on all fronts.

My focus was on mastering the unspoken skills and obtaining these allies. Each time I played the power game, no matter what situation or challenge I faced, my goal was to play my best hand and make power work for me. That meant enrolling players in my career success. Playing the game with unwritten rules means forming relationships with the right people at the right time.

One critical thing I learned was that I had to think about what I could offer those in power to ensure that they would support me and my career goals. This game is not just about being on the receiving end. It is also about having something of value to offer those who support you and ensuring that they recognize what you have to offer. I ultimately relied on the power I held by virtue of the information I had and the unique point of view I could share, and the power I drew from my skill in building and maintaining relationships.

Let me share a story and some insights and lessons that I learned that will hopefully help other Black professional women navigate the power game.

Power in Action

I had been summoned to Dorian's office by his administrative assistant. And as I sat down, pulling out my notebook so I could take a few notes, he cut right to the chase and said, "They need to go." The person he was speaking of who needed "to go" was Stacy, and Stacy reported to me.

You would think that something like that would be my decision. But given the relationship that I had with Dorian, it was not unusual for him to offer his opinion about my work and my job responsibilities. He was much higher than I was in the organization and my role was to help him succeed. In turn, he was to help me. He lived into this contract by giving me access to information and speaking about my work and my value to the company. He was not a mentor or a sponsor, but we had a strategic relationship that benefited both of us.

I knew exactly who he was speaking about when he said "they need to go." However, I felt that although Dorian had a lot to say that made perfect sense, it was not his decision. He did not have the most pertinent facts and he didn't know the entire situation. I had to make a quick decision because he was not an "I'll get back to you" type of person. He always wanted to hear your point of view in the moment and what you were planning to do immediately.

I had two choices: say yes and agree with him or say no, risking a relationship I had worked hard for. This was not just about meeting his request. We needed each other to be successful, and he was leveraging his relationship with me to influence events according to his judgment. He clearly had the upper hand, even though he needed the relationship with me to stay strong. My contribution to the relationship went beyond the organization and impacted his sphere of influence outside work. What I brought to the relationship allowed me to have a degree of influence even though I was lower on the organizational chart.

We rarely disagreed, but this was one time when we did. I acknowledged his points and perspectives, then shared my thinking and my actions. I explained clearly that this was ulti- mately my decision and that I needed him to help me work through the situation. I felt that Stacy had the potential to do more with a little guidance and support. This was not the path of least resistance. At the time it would have been easy to restructure Stacy out of a role since we were going through a reorganization, but I chose not to do that. In a situation where I had less formal hierarchical power, I used the power of my relationship with Dorian to influence the decision at hand.

You may be wondering what was in it for me in this situa- tion. Why was I risking a relationship that I had strategically built to help someone else who was so junior? Stacy had no power. She had little influence in the organization, if any. I could have easily placed her in another job somewhere else in the organization or even ended her employment. But I felt strongly that letting her go was not the right call.

There are defining moments in any career and this was one for me. Ultimately, Dorian listened to me and agreed to support my thinking. Most important, when this occurred, I realized that I had the right voice, a voice with enough power, in my organization not only do what was important for me but also to help others. I know for a fact that Dorian supported me and my power play during our discussion not because he agreed with me or because I was able to persuade him: he still fundamentally disagreed with me. My success was the result of my relationship with Dorian and the power I brought to the discussion. I had a long track record of accurately assessing the organization's talent, and Dorian trusted me. That credibility and trust within this relationship is what gave me power, despite being Dorian's junior in the organizational hierarchy.

I believe that as a leader you have the responsibility to share your power (i.e., lend your voice) to help position others who may not have such an opportunity. This was about ensuring that someone else was given a chance to be successful and positioning them for that success. The only path at that moment was to use my power to influence where I could, even though the other player was much more senior than me and the person I was trying to help.

I took a risk that day because Dorian not only had the power to dismiss my judgment about what Stacy needed, he also had the power to dismiss me. My reputation was on the line, as was my career and all that I had worked for.

I didn't lose any of those things. What I gained was validation of the power of my voice and how I could use it to help others.

The key is about knowing when, how, and with whom to use your power. Knowing who the power players are in your organization is vital to your professional success. Nurture those relationships over time because they will become essential to your career advancement.

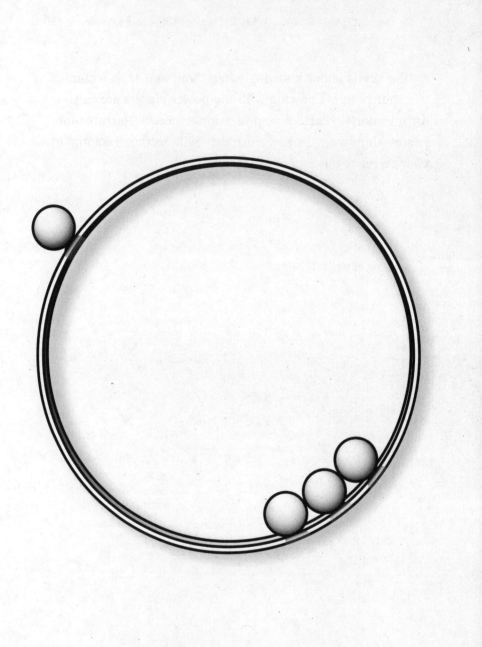

PART TWO

Your Voice, Your Choice

CHAPTER THREE

Stop Cleaning Up the Room

I once heard a colleague say, "When you're in the picture, you sometimes can't see the frame." Often the way you see yourself is not the way your organization sees you. The brand that you think you have may not be the brand you actually have.

As a Black professional woman in the workplace, our brands are often created for us before we get to create them. I often share this story to reinforce what I mean. Imagine two women given the task of crossing the street. On the other side is a group of people observing the two women, waiting for them to join them. They will each be asked to introduce themselves to the group once they arrive. One woman is white and the other woman is Black.

The white woman gets across the street and introduces herself to the group. She shares who she is, what she does, what she stands for, what she believes in, her experiences, and so forth. When the Black woman makes it across the street, she does the same thing. The difference is those who are waiting to hear her story have already created one for her in their minds. They have written her story before she even began to share it. Her task becomes not sharing who she is, but dismantling the myths about her based on the group's preconceived notions and stories about her. They formed their own stories about her as she was walking across the street, before she had the chance to tell her own story. The "opportunity" the Black woman got was to either live their story about her or demonstrate that she wasn't who they believed her to be.

As a Black professional woman, your story is often crafted for you before you have the opportunity to tell it. Know this and understand that you have to be aware that this is the reality. Many leaders in positions of power have never worked with someone like you. They have probably had little if any social experiences with folks like you and they have had very little exposure to others like you, either within the workplace or outside work. The sad reality is that they may even feel that they have no reason to learn about Black people.

I found this to be true in many of the remote locations where I worked. This is why the brand that you bring into the places that you work and the actions that you take become so important. You have to manage the perceptions of those you align yourself with or even those who report to you.

Perception Is More Important Than Intention

In one of my leadership roles, a woman named April reported to me. The organization knew she was super smart; she excelled in many areas. That was her brand, but it wasn't good enough to position her as a future leader. She was trusting and loyal to a fault, often placing others before herself. Her performance was unparalleled. She worked hard and delivered more than the task or project required and she always looked out for me. She had the ability to speak to leaders in a way that made them listen with focus. I was a huge advocate of her success.

However, the leaders of our organization, my peers, did not see all of those amazing qualities. Outstanding performance wasn't enough to move April beyond her current level into a leadership role. Others could not see what I saw, but I needed them to support April.

I wanted to understand what I was missing and to ensure that I wasn't viewed as a leader who could not assess my team members appropriately. My reputation was also on the line; I didn't want to be viewed as someone who was so focused on April's success that I couldn't see what my peers saw. So I dug deeper to see what blind spot I might have.

I started observing April closely in meetings and in her interactions with others. I watched and listened to how what she said was being received by those who were listening to her answers to questions. I also started paying attention to nonverbal behaviors in the meetings we both attended. I even asked peers whom I trusted what they saw and what it was that I wasn't seeing. They recounted exactly what I saw, but they still could not see April as a future leader in our organization.

Then I asked one leader, Marc, to share one word that would describe her. I had assumed that my peers always appreciated the feedback or discussion when April spoke. His response surprised me. What he said was "helper." In the interactions he witnessed, he always saw her in a supporting role. April was helping not only me but also others, and she always appeared to wait for permission from me. He even told me that he had seen her straightening up the room after a meeting. He said that he valued her opinion and that she always had great insight, but he clearly saw her in a secondary position, not a leadership role.

Marc went on to to say that leaders are expected to show a certain presence, a confidence, even if they are not yet in a leadership role. April's brand was not one of a future leader because she didn't demonstrate any confidence and she always acted in support of me and what I said in the meetings—she followed me. Right or wrong, this brand and the narrative about her had already been created. It was ultimately up to her to change the narrative and the view of her within the organization. She needed to own creating that power for herself. My responsibility as her manager was to coach her and to position her in front of the right leaders so they had the opportunity to see her brand. But ultimately it needed to be April's voice that determined her brand. It's your own voice that will give you the power over how people perceive you.

This feedback was valuable. I had been observing what April delivered, not how she delivered it and how it was perceived by those who received it. The term helper stuck in my mind. Then I observed her helping one day. After a meeting, several of us were standing around discussing additional items. I call this the meeting after the meeting. Although technically informal, these meetings are crucial for understanding what might really be going on within a leader's business unit. What I noticed was that although she was present, she wasn't engaged in any conversation. She was straightening up the chairs, throwing away items that had been left on the table, and so forth. She was cleaning up the room.

I immediately had a conversation with her. I asked her why she cleaned the room after the meetings. Her response was that she was just helping out by making the room tidy for others who would use the room next. She was unaware that this behavior might be perceived in a way that reflected negatively on her. I asked her to stop being the individual who always straightened up the room after the meeting, especially meetings where leaders and executives were present, because *helper* was quickly becoming her brand. Your brand is not just what people know about you or what they say about you, it often comes down to what they see you doing—your nonverbal behaviors. Nonverbal behaviors can sometimes speak even more loudly than what you say verbally. In this case, April's actions were speaking volumes.

I explained to her that while cleaning up was a thoughtful gesture, it wasn't what she wanted to be known for or be remembered for. I told her that she was not responsible for cleaning up after others and that she did not want to signal to the organization that she was the junior person in the room. I told her that others were taking note of her behavior. I instructed her to get up after the meeting was over and leave with the other leaders or join an "after the meeting" conversation. This was about positioning herself and not having a story crafted about her based on her actions.

As a leader, I also owned some of the responsibility for this because it became my role to position her as more of a leader than a helper. I told her that I appreciated that she always had my back and was always aligned to what I wanted or needed but that I wanted her to excel beyond that.

It is important to ensure that your leader doesn't always place you in the shadows behind them. Ask for opportunities and assignments that will provide you with the visibility and access you need to demonstrate your leadership qualities. Also remember that you need to ask the people you work with and your manager or his manager how the organization actually sees you. How do they view you and where could they see you going with your professional career? They don't have to answer with a job title; let them describe the role they see you in. And ensure that you are asking the right people, not just anyone. Ask those who will have or could have an impact on your future career.

It's Up to You

Fortunately for April, I supported her and took proactive action on her behalf by investigating what I was missing as a leader. The issue was not what she saw but what she didn't see. Managers often don't think about or take the time to find out what the organization says or believes about their team members except during annual talent reviews. Her demonstration of thoughtfulness and consideration for others was not what the organization valued. The perception others have of you is not something you should passively leave to other people to come up with. You need to take proactive steps to ensure that the right people have an impression of you that will help you achieve your goals.

Many of us continue to stall in our careers because we are not given honest feedback. Many of those in power have no need to share and do not think it is important to share what they think. The secret to my success was that I approached the people who made the decisions within my organizations and asked them how I was perceived, beyond how well I performed. I would explain that I wasn't focused on the feedback I was getting in the form of merit increases and bonuses. I was clear on my level of contribution, but performance alone wasn't what would get me to the next level. I was focused on reaching senior leadership positions. What I wanted to hear was whether it was possible to move my career where I wanted to go. I needed to know if the people who had influence over my career saw that as possible.

How did I start these conversations? First I watched and listened to ensure that I was asking the right individuals. I didn't speak to randomly chosen people. I determined my criteria each year and thought through who could help me reach my goals. Many times it was the same group of leaders or executives. I always included both my functional and operational leaders. I made sure they saw my progress over time and my reputation with them grew.

My conversations were never a surprise to them because I was very clear about my intent. And if I received the runaround from a person I had on my list, that was a message in itself. I made note of that but kept moving forward.

I began these discussions by asking how the organization viewed me. Then I navigated to the uncomfortable question— how the person I was speaking to viewed me. I asked people I trusted and people I didn't trust, people I knew to be huge advocates of my work and people who weren't. Keep in mind that while every leader in your organization may not be powerful, they all have a point of view. Sometimes the person who is not as obvious to you is the one who has the most influence over your career and will have a point of view about you that could help you or hinder you. So make sure that you pay attention and ask wisely. Learn who really makes the career decisions about you in your organization, because it's not just your manager.

Watch who always shares a perspective about someone even when they aren't asked. Watch the person everyone listens to, even when what they say seems to come out of nowhere.

Being proactive about how I was perceived was not just about getting individual pieces of feedback. I also wanted to send a message to the organization that I wanted to and expected to be promoted but that I needed help to get there. Each year, I set up career conversations in January. I used my voice and my actions to communicate that I expected to be promoted. It is important to set the tone and manage your own narrative and be prepared at all times.

What are you known for in your organization? What do you observe about others who are where you would like to be? If your goal is to be seen as a strategic thinker so you can move into business development, share your ideas in meetings. Talk about your ideas openly, and ask others for feedback on those ideas. If your goal is to lead projects, start by asking your manager for opportunities to lead small projects. Use your voice to tell other people what you want so they have the opportunity to help you achieve your goals. Ask for learning opportunities that align with your specific goals. If you leave this up to others, you are losing out on the opportunity to ensure that you are going in the direction you want. You might end up spending valuable time and energy on projects that move you further away from where you want to go.

It is equally important to make sure you are pursuing your goals within the context of your organization's goals. Follow the news about major projects or organization-wide initiatives and volunteer for responsibilities to support those projects. When building relationships with leaders, listen to what they say with the aim of discovering what it is that they care about. Ask about things they seem to care about. When you identify a match between your goals and theirs, ask how you can help with their goals and aspirations. Even if the end goal is not identical to yours, you may be able to gain experience you'll need for your goals in service of theirs. As you are building your career, showing leaders that you are engaged with their goals and the organization's goals is what will ultimately help you achieve yours.

Preparing yourself means positioning yourself for the best career outcomes by letting others in positions of leadership and power in your organization know about your aspirations. You need to communicate to them what your expectations are. Don't assume they will guess or come to these conclusions on their own. Does this mean that you may have to think through how you interact with those in the room? Do you need to consider your actions beyond what you deliver from a performance perspective? Will you run into unconscious and conscious bias? Will you experience microaggressions? Will your race play a part in this? Will those in positions of power within your organization more than likely be white men? The answers to all these questions are an emphatic yes!

The way to combat this is to continually enroll the support of those who make decisions about you. Think strategically. Put your personal business plan in place just as you've been taught to tackle a business issue at your organization. The same principles apply. Most important, do not let those in power off the hook in terms of developing you and helping you craft the right brand for your organization. Hold them accountable.

Ask them not only how they view you, but also ensure that you are having ongoing dialogue about this. You also need to go beyond your manager and ask others you trust to observe you in action. Make sure they see you as you see yourself and how you want to be seen. Again, having advocates across the organization is crucial for your professional success because you cannot rely on just your manager to advocate for you.

Managing and controlling your professional brand is an integral part of your career strategy. Let your brand be the story that you have chosen, not what someone within your organization chose for you. Once you are truly clear about what your brand is and it is what you want others to know about you, you will have a platform for engaging in meaningful relationships. This is a revolving process: having a brand that everyone recognizes ensures that you will be able to build the right relationships with people who can help you, both within and outside your organization. And in turn, those relationships then become the conduits through which you can actively manage and cultivate that brand. You need to ensure that your reputation is that of someone who brings value to your organization. This is how careers are built, and that is the source of your true power.

CHAPTER FOUR

What Is This Job Really Preparing Me For?

No one ever said that climbing the corporate ladder was easy.

By the time I finally became a vice-president, I'd worked hard for every minute of the eleven years since I had completed my first graduate degree. I had what I often refer to as "corporate scar tissue," the marks of the journey.

I was an overachiever. But I am not alone. Many Black women are ready to lead and have been ready for some time. Most people really start to think about leadership around mid-career, from what I've seen and experienced. Unfortunately, when we get to our first jobs, we are told that we need to focus on our deliverables; that is, whatever we are being paid to do. We need to do that exceptionally well.

That is true, but we aren't told the other half of the equation. As we do these jobs to build our careers, we should always be using our voice, asking ourselves and our mentors, "What is this job preparing me for?"

In order to know what your jobs are preparing you for, you have to declare your professional destiny before you get there—ideally as soon as possible. You may not know exactly what you want to do, and what you want to do may change over time. That is what life is all about! I am not speaking of a title or specific job responsibilities or a particular time frame, but you do need to think about your general direction.

For example, I never knew I wanted to be a vice-president of anything or even spend two decades working in corporate America. But I did know that I wanted to be in charge of something. The careers I saw modeled in my extended family were those of entrepreneurs and educators. These were noble professions, but my family members made very little money for all the work I saw them do. In addition, they were always working more than one job at a time in order to make ends meet.

Being an entrepreneur sounded exciting because I saw that you could be in charge of something. However, my family pointed me toward college and made it clear that getting my degree was a foregone conclusion. No one asked my opinion; my mother and father saw college as essential for my success.

When I got to college, I had no idea what I wanted to major in. I thought it might be journalism, but I ended up in business communications after a lot of twists and turns. I fell into the business sector. But what was more important, I stuck to the thought that whatever I was going to do, I wanted to be in charge, I wanted to lead it. So I worked hard at being in charge of everything that I did at work from the beginning, whether it was a team project or an individual assignment. I wanted to own having the ultimate responsibility for getting something done.

Career Conversations

Using your voice to control your image and influence how people perceive you is one of two important ways in which you should be leveraging the power of your voice. Initiating conversations is a powerful tool that can move you forward in your career. The other is to take proactive steps to manage your own career. You need to be initiating and pursuing conversations, not waiting for them to come to you.

I wasn't always sure what being in charge meant in the corporate world until I was having a networking lunch with a senior leader named Valerie. She asked me, "What do you stand for? What do you really want to achieve, Francine, when you come to work every day? What do you stand for that makes that happen?"

I had no clear answer. I wanted to say, "I come to work every day, do what my boss tells me to do, then go home and I get paid two weeks later." It was that simple to me at the time, but that was not a good enough answer from someone who had proclaimed to others that she wanted to lead.

As I was thinking through a better answer, a lot of other things came to mind. But rather than risk giving her a long answer and sounding like I really wasn't clear or didn't know what I was talking about, I told her that I wanted to think about her question and reply later. That gave me a great opportunity to establish a relationship with Valerie. She was very senior and had a lot of power in the organization. I knew that people listened to her and did what she said, so I didn't want to sound clueless.

That day I learned that if you can't reply to an important question, it is better to not say anything and commit to give a response later. Your response needs to be intentional and carefully considered. This is a rule I still live by today. I later learned, although I didn't realize what I was doing at the time, that I was using my voice to strategically manage my career. I recognized that Valerie appeared to want to help me, so I needed to ensure that my reply was well thought out. A strong answer to her question would give me the foundations for a future relationship. Choosing to say that I wanted to think about the question more deeply and circle back helped me continue the relationship. Important questions about you and your career don't need quick answers unless you already know and are confident about what you want to say. Ideally, your answers to such questions should align with what other people in your company want. I hadn't done any of that work beforehand, so telling Valerie that I wanted to be a leader myself was not the right answer. It would have sounded amateurish and naïve. And I had no answer to a possible follow-up question about how I would reach my goal. It was good that I at least knew to defer my answer to the question.

Whenever you are preparing to speak to individuals about yourself and your career or when you are just giving them the chance to get to know you, do your homework as early as possible. Always know as much as possible in advance about anyone you are going to talk with about your career, but also come prepared with answers about yourself and your goals.

Don't forget to be clear about your organization's culture regarding professional development. Every organization will have a specific approach, so make sure that you understand and know what that culture is. Some will value trainings and courses. If this is the approach, you will need to ensure that you are being sent to trainings. If you realize you are not, leverage your relationships and ask what you can do to be considered for such opportunities. Other organizations will value on-the-job training. They will want to give you stretch assignments and see how you do. In this case, ask for these assignments and be sure to proactively request feedback on your performance. And if what you want is not what the company offers, your focus should be looking for work at another company rather than trying to earn a promotion at your current company.

Although I wasn't prepared to answer her question, I knew that Valerie wanted to understand who I was and how I would fit in the company's future. She wanted to know what value I could add, not just to the company but also to her. Powerful leaders don't just do things for the company; they think about themselves. I was also told that she liked to know how a person thought through things. I had learned these things about her by asking people about her before I met with her.

Never have a meeting with someone, especially a meeting about your career, when you don't know something about the person you are meeting with, no matter what level they are. Don't waste your time and theirs by using the meeting to learn about what college they attended, for example, or their career path. You can learn these details on LinkedIn and you should do that research before you meet with them. You can even ask trusted colleagues what you should know about someone before you meet with them. Learn about a person's career and understand what kind of power that they have in the organization. Know who their team members and direct reports are and what their track record of developing and promoting others is. Before you meet with them, think through exactly what you want them to know about you as a member of their organization. Be prepared to discuss something that is important to them and weave yourself into the conversation: your career, what you want them to know about you, and what is important to you.

So when Valerie asked me what I stood for, I was well informed enough to know that she wasn't asking me about my value system or what I believed in. This is the usual way people use the term "stood for," and I could easily have misinterpreted her. Valerie was asking me what I stood for on behalf of the organization. She did not want a monologue on Francine's Core Values. Being able to correctly interpret her question and give her the answer she really wanted was a critical step in proving to her I was leadership material. It is an example of one of the unspoken skills I refer to throughout this book: know the question behind the question.

How did I know the true meaning of her question to me? I knew her team members and direct reports, her track record of developing and promoting others, and I had asked them what she valued. When you contemplate having meetings with people in your organization to talk about your career, make a list of questions about what you need to know about those people and do your research until you know the answers to each item on the list. Have your message well prepared and well thought through. Be comfortable saying that you'll get back to them if they ask you something that you can't answer in the moment. It is better to come back later with a strong response because that will ensure that you are delivering the message that you want. It also puts you in a position of power because you will be able to state your goal in clear, succinct terms.

And whether you are just entering the workforce or are at the end of a stellar career, always understand what any role is preparing you for in the context of the career goal or outcome that you want. Enrolling multiple stakeholders in your career plan is important. I wanted career opportunities that would give me the opportunity to lead. That was my consistent goal.

No matter what job I took on or what opportunities people in the organization spoke to me about, I had in the back of my mind that my next step needed to be one in which I was leading or had the opportunity to lead. I shared that goal with others as well. I wanted people to think of me the way I wanted to be thought of.

Ask the right questions; influence the right narrative about you by volunteering your thoughts, especially when you are asked for them. Know what you are being prepared for and know what you are *not* being prepared for. The only way to know this is to ask those in power what the organizations plans are for your career. Ensure that you receive a clear answer. And remember, keep what you want to do as your number one priority, regardless of whatever answer you hear from those in your organization.

Now Let's Talk about Your Boss

Your manager is the person you have to rely on most. They are the person you usually have the most contact with and receive the most direction from. More important, they are the person the organization assigns to speak about how well your performance aligns with your goals and your career potential. But their ability to assess you correctly as it relates to what's next for you is often where the problem lies. You cannot leave all of this up to the manager; you need to initiate conversations to find out what they think of you and ensure that their assessment of you and their goals for you align with your own. If you leave this up to them, it's their idea of your career that you will end up having, rather than the career you plan for yourself.

I've been in the room when a manager was clueless about how to speak about one of their direct reports. They had not done their homework to understand what they knew about their direct report and to put that knowledge in the context of the organization's goals. As a leader myself, I know that my word about my direct reports counted, but it was always good to have other leaders in the room who could support my thinking and assessment. Most managers and leaders go in on their own and speak about only what they know or believe about you. More than likely, they won't have asked you what your goals are or what your thinking is on an issue that's important to the organization.

This style of management can be risky for a manager's direct reports. When managers describe the people who work under them, they either have the support of the organization or those in the meeting or they don't. When they haven't done the work to learn about your goals and make sure that other people in the room know who you are, they end up standing alone in terms of you and your career opportunities. I've rarely been in a meeting where the people in power were unclear about their position on someone's potential or their future career. If such leaders are not clear about a person's career aspirations or if they do not agree about that person's potential, they will quickly move on.

It's great if your immediate manager has the power to make career decisions about you on their own. But more than likely they won't have that kind of power. Everyone answers to someone else in any organization and managers are no exception. They have to justify their decisions, especially as they relate to promotions. Often it comes down to whether your manager needs approval from others for any given decision and the degree of power and influence they have in the organization. You should always know how much power your manager has. The less power they have, the more buy-in and support they have to garner from others to help you advance your career.

Can your direct manager become an obstacle to your success? The answer is an unqualified yes.

We've all had those career feedback discussions with our managers that yielded very little or nothing at all to help us grow in our current position or prepare us for the next career move. We've all heard the following from a manager somewhere in our career:

> "You're doing a great job and the organization thinks a lot of you."

> "We need to work on developing a robust developmental plan for you."

> "Sit tight and wait it out. You're ready; it's about timing. Your time is coming."

I've heard them all and I'm sure you have heard a few yourself. These are weak statements. The only thought in my mind when people tried some of them with me was, "You're kidding me, right?" But my verbal response was often, "That's great, now let's talk about what that means."

I tell everyone that feedback is a gift and that I love to accept gifts, but I love them even more when they are useful. Don't let a manager get away with a broad response to your questions about career development. Treat the discussion about you just as you would the discussion about the quantitative or financial goals you have committed to as a part of your performance. Think of it this way: your development plan always needs to be robust. It has to be meaningful to you and to your organization.

A Systematic Approach

While controlling the narrative and managing how you are perceived is the most important and most overlooked aspect to career advancement, ensuring that your performance is unimpeachable is also vitally important. This must be in place in order for the more subtle tactics of relationship building and your reputation management to do their work.

Always make sure that your development plan is tied to the business outcomes of your organization. They should always be measurable for the current year.

It is nice to work on very long term or even future projects, but that isn't a winning strategy for your immediate career development. In corporate America, you are only as good as the work the business needs to complete *this year*. Don't sign up for a five-year project if the value of your contribution won't be clear for five years. When the project is over, it will be five years too late for the company to consider you as someone who could take on a position with more responsibility. When considering term projects, make sure there are sub-deliverables that will allow you to demonstrate your value in concrete ways within six to twelve months of signing on. Ensure that you are monitoring your career year-over-year and making decisions that will move it along.

I made it my personal mission to speak with my direct manager every three months. I started in January every year. I would begin the conversation by saying, "Welcome back. I hope you had a restful holiday. It was awesome to have time to enjoy my family and have some personal time and a break from professional tasks. But I also had time to think about my career without the distraction of all of the work deliverables. Specifically, I had time to think about what is next for me and how I can ensure that I am prepared as we head into this year. I want to get off to a good start and I need your feedback and to know your thinking about that. I am confident that you want me to get off to a great start this year."

When I met with my manager again in early April, the conversation was: "I know that you are getting ready for the company talent reviews and I want you to have everything you need to present me in the best light possible to your peers. I want to know how I can help you to prepare. Let's discuss."

In late June or early July, my message was: "We're halfway through the year and I'd like the opportunity to share my progress so far. I'd also like to ask where I should be with my developmental goals at this point in the year. Can I schedule time with you to ensure that we continue to be aligned about my progress?"

The fourth conversation, which was in October, would begin with this statement: "As I wrap up my performance for the year, let's talk about my professional development and whether I am on track. This is what we agreed to at the beginning of the year [share what was decided in your January meeting]. Here is my progress on those goals. I want to ensure that what I have been working on and the results I have demonstrated will ensure a successful close to the year."

While this is time consuming, it doesn't leave room for your manager to tell you that you are "doing a good job" and then drop the conversation. It holds your manager accountable. It will help you avoid being surprised to discover that your career is not going anywhere. It allows you to prevent being on the receiving end of someone else's perspective in a situation where you cannot respond until after the damage has been done. It also puts your manager on notice that you are serious about your career and your development and that you expect that they will help you succeed. Being on top of your career discussions places you in the power position regarding your career path. It ensures that you and your manager have the right discussions and build the right relationship beyond your standard performance reviews. It lets you know along the way what you need to do. It signals to both your manager and your organization that you are serious about advancing in your career.

If you wait for permission to have discussions about your career or until the designated time when your organization has such discussions with their employees, it will be too late. Your career growth and development is not a once-a-year conversation, whether you are speaking to your direct manager or others. Seek out the leaders you want to enroll in your career growth. This is about getting the career you want and shifting the power toward you.

Playing the Hand You've Been Dealt

Often, we can't select our managers. But you always need to know how your manager is viewed in the organization you work for. In other words, know what your manager is capable of doing or not doing. Always know if your manager is in a position of influence and power in your organization. Do they understand the unwritten rules of your organization regarding your career or your advancement? Do they know how the organizational structure really works in your company? There is always a formal organizational chart and an informal one. Sometimes those who truly have power in your organization aren't at the top of the organizational chart. Where does your manager fall on the informal organizational chart? Does your manager really understand how things get done?

Can your manager help you avoid pitfalls or protect you if something unexpected about you comes up that could have a negative impact on your career? You may have to rely on others and their insights if your manager is not a power player. Those relationships can be invaluable in terms of providing information that you need to protect your career. One time a leader told me in confidence that they could no longer protect me when he found out about something from his own network. In that situation, at least I had warning and I knew what my options were.

Even if a manager you report to is a very senior leader or executive who doesn't have to consult with anyone when they make decisions about you and your career, they usually won't make such decisions alone. They won't want to take that risk. I have worked for powerful leaders and executives who always have a clear opinion about the people on their team. They always have a perspective on almost everything, including the organization's talent. But they will listen to other leaders, especially those they trust.

Your manager can be in a powerful position and have a powerful title but have no power in the organization. Obviously, regardless of how much power your manager has, don't discount them. They can sabotage your progress or at a minimum slow it down. The key is for you to be clear about what you want to achieve in terms of your professional development. Ensure that your manager knows the message you want them to have about you and is equipped to share that message in conversations with other leaders about your career and moving you to the next level. The way to do this is to constantly inform your manager about your career plans. This relationship is one that you need to manage proactively. Your manager is crucial for your career success even when they don't appear to support you.

However, you should also ensure that you are building relationships with other leaders who have true authority and who thus will be well placed to support you. Soliciting feedback and obtaining insights from others in your organization will play a vital role in your overall career success because it will enlist individuals who can speak on your behalf and know enough about you to speak about you. If I had not had leaders in the room during a talent review where I was characterized as not "playing nice" with others, I don't know where my career would have led. I am thankful for those other leaders who stood up for me. The saving grace for me was that those leaders collectively had more legitimate power and credibility in the organization than my direct manager. I had spent time nurturing relationships with them and delivering on their objectives and company goals. I never knew that I would need this type of support and you probably never will either. But don't ever forget to at least think about the possibility that you will need support from people other than your manager. Always take inventory of who is in your power circle and think about how they can help you if you ever need external support.

CHAPTER FIVE

To Be
or Not
to Be
Authentic

A uthenticity. When I hear this term, I immediately think to myself, "Enough of an overused term with underexplored meaning." I do not intend to take anything away from the topic of authenticity, as it is king right now in career development literature. The workplace is changing and we as professionals are evolving as well. Organizations are telling its employees to feel free to be authentic, that it's OK to bring your whole self to work.

Authenticity goes both ways. I often wonder whether those who are telling us to be authentic at work are doing that themselves. How much do you really know about your direct manager? How much do you know about the leaders in your organization? Are you seeing their real selves?

Do the people who write about authenticity really understand what they are asking employees to do? Do they understand the context of what it means to bring everything about who I am, what I stand for, what I believe in, what I care about, how I live my life, and so many other facets of my personhood into the workplace? Are organizations truly ready for that?

My response is a resounding "no."

Black Women and Authenticity at Work

For any career woman, especially a Black professional woman, bringing her authentic self to the workplace without understanding the consequences of doing so in her specific organization is a huge risk to her career, especially if her objective is to advance into leadership. From my perspective, the workplace as it exists today is not ready for authenticity. We have not defined what authenticity means in the context of a professional career.

What many have failed to understand about authenticity is that it's not a simple issue. Creating an authentic workplace requires a lot of forethought, and the hard work is something everyone has to do for themself. It can't be a one-size-fits-all solution. Being authentic at work is a very personal issue. You need to think about how authentic you want to be with others in your company in the context of your professional career goals. This is not about what the organization tells you what they would like you to do. This is about what you will accept or choose to do, what you choose to share about yourself. To be authentic means to be very personal, especially in the workplace.

There will be those in positions of leadership and authority who have the best of intentions when asking us to bring our authentic selves to the workplace. However, they may get it totally wrong despite their efforts to help us. In fact, authenticity in the workplace often backfires, even in a workplace that claims to welcome it. All help is not good help.

Authenticity has everything to do with the message you want to convey and the stage you want to set for what people at work know about you, especially those who have the power to make decisions about your career. For you to have a good experience with authenticity at work, the receivers of your authenticity must be open and savvy enough to process that information—to understand you. But as a Black woman, those receiving your experience will find what you are offering to be counterintuitive and foreign to what they have experienced in their own lives. Know that they will likely interpret your expression of your authentic self through the lens of their own, different experiences. For Black women, this is often problematic. Many people at work will lack the context for how to interpret your self-expression because they take many things for granted about the workplace—things they have not thought about simply because they have not had to. There's a saying that "privilege is invisible to those who have it." This is not necessarily because they don't want to see the obstacles Black women encounter; it's often because they are working with what is in front of them and paying attention to things that will maximize their own career.

The most important factor here is that there are so few Black women in positions of leadership and authority in the rooms with most of our leaders. There are few opportunities for white leaders to get to know us over time and many leaders don't prioritize doing so. Although we are told that leaders want to learn about who we truly are, that we are given permission to bring our whole selves to the workplace, it often doesn't benefit Black women to take those leaders at their word.

There are unique risks to Black women for bringing their more authentic selves to the workplace. Since there are fewer of us, the possibility that we will be misinterpreted is large. People who don't have personal experience with our cultures are much more likely to stereotype us than to authentically see us. People will assume things about us incorrectly. Those incorrect assumptions can have a devastating impact on a career.

The harsh reality is that the negative stereotypes in our culture about Black women will follow you into even the most enlightened workplace. I've seen many times how the assessment of Black women boils down to "She's great, but..." Or "She's talented but I just don't see her [as leadership material]." Someone's negative stereotype of you as a Black woman may result in your being assigned to projects that don't allow you to demonstrate your potential. Informality simply does not work for Black women the same way it works for white men. Instead of setting you apart and distinguishing what is unique about you, you'll end up with a brand that is created for you by others' misconceptions, rather than a powerful brand created by you.

What Does Authenticity Even Mean?

We often don't think about which situations are appropriate for authenticity and which are not. There are times when a situation does not call for or require our authenticity. That doesn't mean that you are not being true to others about who you are. The term code-switching refers to the practice of presenting one facet of your persona for one audience and another part of your persona for another. This simply means knowing the environment and situation you are in and being clear about how you want to respond based on the goals you are trying to achieve. Code-switching is a perfectly appropriate method for deciding which pieces of yourself you want to show and does not make anyone less authentic.

Your authenticity is very personal. You need to consider the relationships you have with the receivers and who they are. You have to trust them and they have to trust you. Like all relationships, your connections with people at work require time and investment from both parties.

Therein lies the problem with authenticity at work that no training at work will fix. Many companies try their best by commissioning diversity workshops, hiring equity experts to speak to their organization, or creating campaigns and events to demonstrate that they want employees to feel comfortable, to feel that they belong—that you belong. They want you to feel that you can bring all that you are to the workplace. However, these workshops, campaigns, and events are not where Black women need to start on the topic of authenticity. You need to think more carefully about the messages you want to convey about who you are to the people who are important for your career.

You have to first dig into the reality behind the outwardly expressed values, and only you can do this. Understand what has actually happened to those who have bought their authentic selves to your workplace. You need to observe, investigate, and then decide. Pay attention to the way others around you present themselves and how the organization responds to them. How do colleagues in your organization respond to people who express themselves in a way similar to how you might express yourself? How do leaders perceive them? How does their manager perceive them? How do other managers perceive them? The answers to these questions will give you valuable data about how the organization and its leadership will react to you should you make similar choices.

I'm not talking about the official company line or what is expressed in the official literature. This is about observing what is less obvious. Look at trends: what do you notice about everyone at the most senior, C-suite levels? What about the executive levels? Keep going down the organizational chart and noticing who gets placed where. How do people in these categories present themselves? This kind of assessment will give you invaluable data about what will work while you are trying to get to those levels. If, for example, you would like to come to work with green hair, first consider what happens to those who have green hair. Maybe your organization says they love people with green hair. But if you notice that there are many people with green hair working the secretarial positions, and no one with green hair at the senior levels, you should consider that to be a more genuine reflection of how the organization views people with green hair. Actions and results speak louder than words.

Here are some questions to ask yourself about how you are perceived and what might happen if you suddenly changed your way of being at work. Use the answers to these questions about your leadership to help you determine how much of yourself to show in your workplace:

> Who knows you and your work? What is their level in the organization? What do they think about you?
>
> What do you think comes to mind when your name is mentioned when you are not in the room?
>
> Is your organization truly accepting of you and your brand?
>
> Is that your authentic self?

What about yourself do you feel a desire to share that you have felt unable to share so far?

Do you know if they would be truly accepting of your authentic self?

Have you ever thought about how you want to have others in the organization view you—whether or not that is your authentic self?

Have you thought about what your authenticity would yield for you in your organization?

Based on your observation of the cultural trends in your workplace, would being authentic put you in a better position than where you are now?

These questions can only be answered through investigation. You need to seek those answers and then use your voice to present the version of you that reflects what you want the organization to know about you. Whether that is your authentic self or not is your decision, not the decision of the organization or its leaders. How authentic you are is your professional choice.

Who Are You Talking To?

I've always known that it was important for me to use my voice intentionally to manage any situation I was confronted with, whether I expected it or not. Sometimes it's necessary to assess the level of authenticity that is called for on the fly. Preparation for these moments is critical.

I was wrapping up my day at work when a leader stopped by my office. I was on the phone but my door was open, so I waved for him to come in while I was talking. As I was speaking on the phone, he had his back to me, looking at the pictures I had on another desk. These pictures were of my husband, my son, and my siblings and of interesting places I had traveled to. I changed them every month or so. The pictures often gave visitors something to do and the opportunity to engage in small talk.

After I hung up the phone, I made a lighthearted comment about the fact that they were good conversation starters and said, "They provide a little insight into who I am, since being the HR leader doesn't always make people comfortable." I asked him if he found any of them interesting, since each one had a story behind it.

He didn't answer my question. Instead, he smirked and said, "I know that this is not the true story behind 'Francine' or who she is; this is what you want us to know about you."

I did not speak. I only tilted my head, and looked straight at him. I smiled the same smile that I gave the administrative assistant who had told me to "sit over there." There may be moments in your professional life when you need to assess whether or not to share more about yourself with someone you work with. In this case, his smirk told me everything I needed to know about whether this was a safe moment to share more of my authentic self. The critical thing to do in these moments is to take a mental pause and ask yourself whether it would be beneficial to you to do so. Clearly, in this situation, it would not have been.

First, consider who you are talking to. In the situation I just described, I chose not to share anything about myself. This decision was based not only on his behavior but also on what I already knew about him. I knew him very well. I had watched him and had listened to how he "supported" others. He had a reputation of looking out for himself first and others later. I had already chosen not to trust him.

So that smile I gave him was one that conveyed that he was right. We worked in an environment where sharing all of who you were offered no benefit to your career. I had purposefully chosen to share only what I wanted him to know. Despite how he operated in the workplace, we had a very good working relationship. I chose to take this conversation no further and moved us on to the practical matter that had brought him to my office. What influenced my decision was what I knew about him and what I wanted out of our professional relationship, not about what the organization may or may not have said about authenticity in the workplace. Being authentic is first and foremost about knowing how to read your audience. Who are they and how are they likely to react to your authentic self?

Organizations that encourage authenticity without consideration of the consequences for Black employees want to make it seem simple, but those organizations still have a very long way to go. It's unlikely that the leaders who have stewardship of such organizations have done the work to create a safe environment for all of their employees to be authentic or considered what the professional consequences of authenticity might be for some people.

This Is Not an Excuse, but It Is a Reality

As a Black woman, being your authentic self with anyone involves a certain level of trust and consideration for what the value of doing so might be. As we know, trust occurs over time and it is earned. So trusting an organization and its leadership, specifically your leaders, take that time.

Don't get caught up in the hype that the organization you work within wants to accept the total you and so does its leadership.

In my experience and what I continue to see today is that this works only if you fit (yes, I said the "f" word) within that organization's culture and what it believes is important. Organizations will always say what the world wants to hear. But it is only after carefully observing their actions and who tends to get what opportunity that you will be able to figure out what their real value system is.

You can't control the organization as a whole. You are only one individual and unfortunately you can't shift the thinking of many on a short time frame. Only ever share what you want other people to know about you. Know that people make decisions about you all the time. They will use the information that they know about you to make those decisions. That is just human nature. We work with what we know and your organizations and its leadership are no different.

You can choose who you should and should not be authentic with. This can be challenging, since who you are is who you are. However, there is nothing wrong with making the decision that you are comfortable not sharing everything about who you are. Control your narrative and know the consequences of sharing who you are in your workplace. This is about you understanding your workplace and how you want to position yourself. You have the power to do this, which means you can also manage the consequences.

The Bottom Line

The most important consideration in deciding whether or not to be authentic is what impact doing so is likely to have for you and whether or not that impact will move you closer to your goals. What is the message you want your organization to have about you? Will sharing your authentic self result in others hearing that message? To achieve your bigger goals, you have to know when you can be completely authentic, when you can be somewhat authentic, and when you cannot be authentic at all. The real power of authenticity is in what you chose to communicate and share about yourself and with whom. I encourage you to manage it, as not everyone has the best of intentions for you and your career.

Showing your authentic self, or not, needs to be determined by the relationships that you establish. There is no organizational solution for this or guidelines to follow. Remember to ask yourself: do you know the authentic selves of your leaders or managers? What do you truly know about them? Ensure that you are building relationships on a foundation of mutuality. Be authentic in relationships where you see value in doing so, but always ensure that you are aware of what the consequences of doing so are likely to be in your organization. Consequences may work for you or against you, but it's up to you to know what they are and make your choices accordingly. If you are comfortable and it works for you that the organization sees your authentic self, that is great and you should do it.

Ultimately, you have to discern what is most important to you. You can control how authentic you want to be. Your power is in your voice to manage what people think about you through what you choose to tell them. This is where you have the ability to control the narrative others have about you—that's the true power base from which to manage your authentic self.

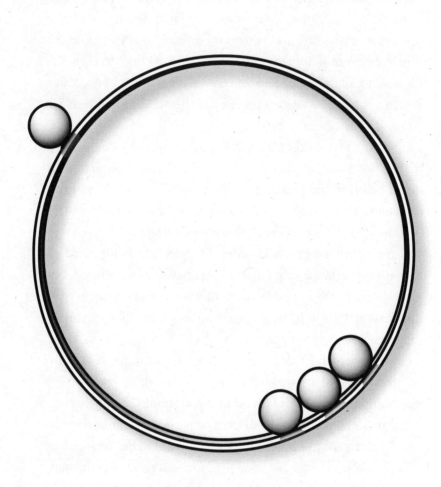

PART THREE

The Relationships That Will Make Power Work for You

CHAPTER SIX

It's Never Too Early to Build a Network

Playing the power game has it risks. Everything that is worth something carries some type of risk. Your career is no different. Some of the risks you take will pay off and some will merely offer you valuable learning experiences. When you are navigating through a risk that didn't pay off, you'll need a professional network to provide guidance, protection, or other opportunities. I define a professional network as a group of people who are focused on building relationships with each other and on leveraging each other's strengths for mutual benefit. This is often transactional and involves sharing resources with the goal of achieving good business results for all involved.

Many of us want to believe that if we work hard and our work yields strong results, our organization will see us as promotable or view us as ready to lead others. But in the power game, that is often not the case. Black women especially run the risk of being labeled as hard workers, which translates as "not strategic enough" in the business world. I've been there myself and have received such feedback. The only things my hard work got for me were more work, larger tactical responsibilities, and assignments with quick turnarounds.

I've had many conversations with employees who told me that they thought that leaders in their organization and their immediate manager had their back. They thought that certain individuals were watching out for them and protecting their best interests when they weren't around to speak for themselves. They were shocked to learn that those people hadn't done either of those things.

They often learned that no one was advocating for them when they didn't receive a developmental assignment they had been working toward even though they had discussed it with their manager or when they didn't receive a promotion, a raise, or even the recognition they deserved. Someone else enjoyed fifteen seconds of company fame. Their performance was outstanding, but the opportunities that were offered to them didn't match their record as an employee. Even worse, sometimes they were sent to a course that purported to be a developmental class but was really about how to be content with where they were because their careers were going no further. Ultimately, someone might even be given a coach that the company had hired to help them reach the conclusion that they needed to move out of the organization. Some learned they were being "absorbed," code for the news that their job was going away, which more than likely meant that they were being laid off.

These stories came from individuals who were outstanding performers but who did not understand the power game.

They hadn't learned how to play their best hand or leverage the power they had to position themselves for career success. And often they had no one in the organization they could go to for guidance, support, or help to get through their current situation.

Networking Is Not Just for Getting a Job

What all of the situations I've described had in common was the absence of a robust professional network. Many people who find themselves in these situations have neglected to continuously nurture and leverage their own professional network. I cannot stress enough how important it is to have the right people to help you navigate within and outside your organization.

I learned that it was very important to watch the people who were being promoted, to notice who they aligned themselves with and who spoke about them openly. I paid attention to how the individuals who were deemed successful navigated within our organizations. Very early in my career, I made sure that the people the organization deemed successful knew about me and what I could offer them.

Early in my career I didn't know that what I was building is what we now call a professional network. I just knew that I needed people in positions of authority and power at work to help me get things done. I knew I had to engage with the people who were being promoted. I live by the belief that success helps success. These individuals were successful and I wanted to be successful too.

My actions and awareness paid off tremendously throughout my career.

It's YOUR Network

A network is one of the most powerful tools in a career arsenal, but it is often taken for granted. People expend energy on other tactics they think might work better than a network or something they have seen work for someone else instead of focusing on cultivating their network. This is a mistake. The power of your network comes from the time you take to nurture and develop the relationships you need to get things done, both within and outside your organization.

The network that you develop through building meaningful relationships is one of the most powerful tools you will have in your career. It is yours to own because you create it. No one will hand you a network and no one but you has the ability to nurture and develop your network by strategically creating the relationships that are aligned with your professional goals. The success of the relationships you choose to create are in your hands and yours alone. Your ongoing power is based on ensuring that the members of your network see the value of a mutual relationship with you.

A robust network is a strong lever for your professional success if you take the time to invest in those who are in it. Just as you are asking them to invest in you, the people you choose for your network want a relationship where you are also investing in them, regardless of their organizational level. The power of a successful network is that as long as you are actively maintaining it, it is always working in the background on your behalf.

Unbeknownst to Me

Building your network is a long game. Sometimes the connections you make will benefit you years after you make an initial connection. I remember sitting across the table from someone who was an intern at my organization at the time. I knew who she was, but I'd had very little interaction with her. We were having lunch with two other colleagues and were discussing the challenges of planning a wedding, as one of the women was about to get married.

My colleagues were quite talkative and we were cutting each other off in our excitement. Each of us had an opinion except the intern. I noticed that she was very quiet and made very few comments. I was puzzled by this, as she was the only person in the conversation who was already married. I wondered why she was not volunteering her expertise.

Building a network has as much to do with informal, personal conversations and connection as it does with your professional responsibilities. I'd already noticed that the intern always had insightful things to say, especially when it related to the project she and my colleagues were working on and what was happening in our work environment. I was intrigued by her thinking; she was clearly very smart. In hindsight, I had a sense that she was going to do great things and I felt that I needed to know her. I knew that she would go forward to do bigger things in her career and I felt that I needed to stay connected to her even after the internship ended. I was hoping to build a relationship with her.

After lunch, I stopped by her office to strike up a conversation. I found out that her wedding had been based on very different rituals and ceremonies. The ceremony that my colleague was describing was not the same as hers had been, so she had been listening and learning as well. We had a wonderful conversation about the many differences in wedding traditions around the world.

Despite the informal, nonwork-related content of our conversation, this moment of connection led to the beginning of our relationship. On the basis of my interactions with her, I offered to be a resource to help her navigate in our organization. I understood the culture of the organization and its leaders; as an intern, she did not have that knowledge yet. I felt that I had something that could help her succeed and that I could also learn from her. I had been working only about three years myself, so I was new to the corporate setting, but I knew that I could help her and she could help me. It's never too early to start building your network; you don't have to wait until you achieve a certain level of success. This relationship paid off tremendously later in my career.

Even early in your career, there will be things of value you can offer to others as a way to build mutually beneficial relationships. I had been told even before I began my career that I had a gift for connecting with people no matter who they were, where they came from, or what they represented. I saw it as something I had to do to ensure that others were comfortable with me in whatever situation I was in. In hindsight I can see that my career was being built as I was growing up. I was being trained for corporate America. I took this talent into the workplace.

My ability to listen intently, distill messages, and interpret information became my currency at work. People knew that I had the ability to help them using these skills and ultimately help them learn to do these things themselves. This later became power that I leveraged throughout my professional career.

I encourage you to think about what you are good at beyond the obvious skills you bring to your job. Most often what you are really good at has nothing to do with work. How can you leverage these gifts and skills in the service of those you want to build relationships with? Relationships start with an offer; how can you help those around you? In my case, my ability to listen intently and with the ability to distill messages and inter-pret information became my organizational currency—people knew I had the ability to help them. Another example might be if you have responsibility for managing the data entry for a company's tech system. You may know how this system works and how to access information more effectively than those senior to you. Your access to this information might be valu-able to a senior leader. Think creatively and don't undervalue what you know.

My brief conversation with the intern taught me a valu-able lesson and started my practice of using my currency and power to achieve my goals. Continuing this practice of infor-mal lunch meetings led to many more conversations with executives and C-suite leaders that I knew had influence and power over my career.

How to Get Time with the C-Suite

One of the most effective tools in my arsenal was purposefully scheduling these lunches with very powerful leaders. I wasn't very senior when I began this. To the contrary, I started doing this quite early in my career. I figured that there was no time like the present to take such a risk. I didn't wait for my boss to introduce me or for an event where I would meet executives to try to get on someone's calendar.

Often it would take a long time to schedule a lunch with one of the leaders I wanted to meet, but I was patient because access to them was important to me. Sometimes I would get a "no" reply or I would hear that the person was "just too busy right now with [insert the excuse] to have lunch to meet with you." My response would be, "OK, please keep me on his calendar and push our meeting forward. I'll check back in a few weeks." It sometimes took up to six months to get a lunch scheduled. I had been given some advice not to give up, that a "no" just means "not right now."

Ultimately, many of the lunches would happen, even when it took months. I quickly learned that these meetings were less about me and more about the person who was talking. The person in power did most of the talking. Typically, the leader or executive who sat across the table from me never looked like me. Even more daunting, we often had no shared experiences. However, I learned that what we shared was that each of us wanted something from the other.

They always asked what I wanted out of the meeting because after all, I had made the request to have lunch with them. I would respond that I wanted to learn about them and how they had succeeded in their career. I was clear that it was not about just repeating their resume. I wanted to truly understand how they had achieved their position. What had they done to build toward their current role and who had helped them? I conveyed the message that I aspired to advance as well. I was looking for insights they could share to help me achieve a level similar to theirs one day.

These exchanges were not just about learning possible road maps for me to follow. They helped me understand who these leaders were and what they wanted. Usually their questions became about who I was and why I wanted to talk to them. It is rare that a business meeting occurs without an exchange of something. I listened to them tell their stories, then I shared mine. I never regarded my lunch meetings as casual discussions. I knew that being prepared and not appearing to waste their time was important. I did my homework to learn about them and their organization, their areas of responsibility, their career achievements, and what they were known for.

I discovered that leaders also wanted to know what I thought about others or specific situations. Despite my being the (sometimes much more) junior person, they would still ask for my perspective on things going on in the organization. Sometimes I felt like it was a test. But it was always a test that I was prepared for. I utilized the skill of observing my environment that I had developed and mastered as a child and shared my thoughts when I was asked for them. The advice my father gave me as a teen as I went off to college was paying off tremendously.

I became known as someone with a strong ability to understand the intentions of others and to provide my insights and thoughts to people in managerial and executive roles. As I became more senior, my ability to correctly assess the actions of others and to think through any implications for the businesses and its leaders became a currency that leaders valued. Those in power wanted a skill that I had and they had something that I wanted: they wanted insight and advice and I wanted to reach an executive level in the organizations I worked for.

In my professional relationships, having access to each other paid off tremendously. I was able to offer valuable insights and perspective into things other people did not understand. Most people think leaders have everything figured out, but in reality, they often do not. They value having trusted relationships with even junior employees. In return for this, those in my network gave me access to places I wouldn't have had access to without them. They supported my initiatives and positioned me for promising opportunities and huge projects that allowed me to concretely demonstrate my value to the company.

Work to ensure that you have something that makes you valuable to people in positions of power. Your particular skill may not be obvious to you, but it is important that you think about this. Even though you may have no shared experiences with managers and executives, you can identify a skill or some form of currency that they want. You need to find out what that is for yourself, and you'll usually need to look beyond just what they say. Also observe their actions and what contributions are actually rewarded with more than just praise. Learn what people in power want and consider what skills you have that could help them get it. What does your organization value beyond the obvious? Find someone in your organization you trust to validate that what you have identified is a skill your organization values.

Over time, many of the leaders and executives I had conversations with became a part of my professional network. Some became members of what I called my power circle. These were individuals who knew me particularly well and who I knew well. I had a closer relationship with them than with every member of my extended network. Some could make decisions about me or could help people who could make decisions about me to decide in my favor. These were people who were willing to put their career on the line for me and speak on my behalf publicly and privately.

These are people who can give you advice, as you will do for them. Your collective currency increases in value as you both achieve your goals. This is the benefit of having such a group on your side as you grow together. Focus on refining the power that you bring over time; that is why it is so important to discover the particular skills you bring as soon as possible. Then you can cultivate them as you ascend in your career. You may not need the people in your power circle for a very long time, but when you need them, you need them. My power circle became invaluable, as I learned at many critical moments in my career.

You Will Always Need Your Network

As your career grows, you will need at least one or two trusted advisors in your power circle and more if you can find them. I was fortunate to have four. There came a point in my career when having spent so many years building these connections proved absolutely crucial to my survival. My organizational advocates supported my work because they knew me and what I stood for. They were often in the rooms where I wasn't and could speak for me if my name came up.

When a powerful executive threatened my job, my power circle came to the rescue. They were able to help me get out of a bad situation. The executive, who was a few levels above me, was clearly using coercive power and their influence to push me out of the organization. They were casting aspersions on my work and my potential, speaking poorly of me to people both in public and in private, in unofficial water-cooler talk, and in official talent development contexts. There are times when you decide a job is no longer serving you and choose to move on. But there will be other situations where you decide the opposite. When you have a job and a role you love, where you see advancement potential, and where you decide to stay and fight. This was one of those times for me.

I had no intention of leaving the company, but I needed help in a big way. The executive who was threatening my job had been known to destroy careers, and I knew that I was going to have to make a big lateral move to get my reporting structure away from their influence.

I also knew that disputing what someone believes or says about you, especially if it isn't true, is often more detrimental to your career and can only makes things worse. This is especially important if they are more senior than you and have more power than you. More important, you will waste precious time disputing them or trying to prove them wrong. Believe me, you'll get nowhere.

I called one executive who knew me and my work and had the power to help me. I shared my story, not necessarily looking for them to do anything but to ask for advice. They went beyond advice and offered me a job. It was a promotion.

That particular member of my power circle was the intern I had befriended years ago.

Know What You Are Playing For

If you don't have a professional network, work on establishing one as soon as possible. If it has been dormant, work on reactivating it. If your network is robust, think about who could be a part of your inner power circle and how to strategically leverage those relationships. Identify who can advocate for you in your organization. This is not just about having a positive relationship with someone; it is about choosing people who can stand and speak for you when things get a little challenging for you or your career is on the line. You don't need a lot of people in the subset of your network that will constitute your power circle, but they need to be people who can help you navigate issues that may arise within your company and, if need be, outside the company.

Building a network of professionals takes time and dedication. And cultivating a true power circle takes even more time. You give as much as you receive. Preparing before you connect with individuals in your current or future professional network is essential to your overall career strategy. Do your research on any person you meet with and know with a high degree of precision what your goals are for the conversation. If you skip this step, your meetings may do more harm than good because you will be leaving the outcome up to chance. And often, such outcomes cannot be fixed or reversed when they don't go as you had hoped. You may not be able to cultivate a strong enough connection with them if you have not thought in advance how to engage and enlist them. The effectiveness of your professional network hinges on whether you have a well-thought-out plan in place before you engage with others. How you plan for your network ultimately determines whether it will work for you. Engaging with your network only when you need to accomplish something (as most people do) is risky. Your success depends on your commitment to be as accountable to your network as you want it to be accountable to you, all the time.

Know what you are playing for to ensure that you will be able to play your best power hand. Know what you are trying to accomplish. What is the result you are trying to achieve with your career? Start with the end in mind. Ask yourself: overall where do you want your career to go? This doesn't have to be a title, but you need to be able to describe it. You need to be able to visualize what success looks like and bring that picture to life as you engage others in your professional success. From there you can back in to a plan for achieving this career goal.

Most people don't think about their career goals until their organization asks them to do so. Then the goal is memorialized on a career document with general steps or actions to take (if you are lucky) without any accountability for follow-through. They discuss this document with their manager and then return to their day-to-day tasks until the next annual career cycle repeats the process. These actions don't do anything to advance your career.

Having clear goals that you own is important. You need to be clear about what your advancement goals are before you share them with anyone. Your network can become a valuable asset to you if you know what you want. The people in your network can confirm if you are on the right track, and they can often help you achieve a particular career goal or even tell you if it's not achievable. If you choose to share your goals with members of your network in order to get preliminary feedback, make sure you have thought through them to the best of your ability. It is always important to give someone something to react to instead of going to them empty-handed.

Also ensure that what you offer to the members of your network makes sense for their needs and for the particular context. Be sure you are offering something that person needs. How do you find out what they need? Ask them! Having clear goals will help you engage and leverage each individual appropriately.

Becoming the Master of Your Network

It takes time to clearly establish your career goals, identify your specific valuable skills, build and maintain a professional network, and position your network as a part of your overall plan to advance. You must ask yourself whether you are willing to make the investment.

Having lunch with senior leaders and executives gave me access that I normally wouldn't have had to individuals who often made decisions about me. But having a well-thought-out plan meant that my conversations with those people were deeper. These meetings reinforced what I wanted from myself and what I expected from the organizations I worked for.

Connecting with the right players in your network without being prepared to play your best power hand hinders your success. A good plan helps you chart a course of action but is also flexible enough to make any necessary adjustments. More important, it will help you get the results you want rather than leaving the course of your career up to chance. Get your plan ready and prepare to meet the players in your organization.

CHAPTER SEVEN

Who's Pounding on the Table for You, Francine?

"Who's pounding on the table for you, Francine?"
This is one of the funnier questions I've been asked in my career, but I knew what this senior leader, who I'll call Sam, meant. What he meant was, who would speak up for me? Who would not only support my work but also support me as an individual in our organization? In other words, Sam was asking me who my sponsor was. At the time, I didn't have the answer I should have.

I took too long to answer, which is often viewed in the corporate world as a weakness, especially since I was a senior leader. What was ironic was that I'd sat in many meetings at the leadership table where I discussed individuals and had often asked myself who a person's sponsor was. In those contexts, I was the one asking, "So who supports [insert the name]?" Or, "Who in the organization is supportive of [insert the name]? When I asked this question, everyone in the room knew that I was asking the same thing Sam was now asking me: Who would stand up for me and risk their career if I needed that level of help?

Sponsorship

Having a powerful person in your organization who can speak about you and who supports you and your professional development is critical to your career advancement. With sponsorship comes trust and credibility. A sponsor will do more than just position you to get a big promotion or a key assignment. Most people understand the word sponsor to mean someone who would be willing to put all that they have worked to professionally achieve on the line for you. However, this is only half of the equation.

A healthy relationship with a sponsor is reciprocal. In exchange for the professional and personal credibility a sponsor uses on your behalf, the person being sponsored works to ensure that they are the person the sponsor says they are and that they deliver in the roles the sponsor has positioned them for. This relationship is about your reputation as much as it is about your sponsor's reputation. You and your sponsor both have to be trustworthy and honest with each other. That is what being in a sponsoring relationship is all about. You both own and share in the power you both gain from the connection with each other.

We also know that it takes a long time to build trust, but it can take only a second to lose it. A sponsorship relationship takes time and is built on both your actions and theirs. If someone is sponsoring you, it means that you both believe in and have committed to each other, and, most important, that you both trust each other.

Your Sponsor Probably Won't Look Like You

At this point in time, the people who are in positions of leadership and authority in many institutions don't look like us. This is our reality now and it may be our reality for some time, even after we get to the leadership and executive level.

As a Black woman, you are dealing with people in power in your workplace who likely have had no experience of you or common experiences with you. They say they want to be allies, but they often don't know how to do that and all the training in the world won't get them there. Telling people in power that they are required to sponsor Black women or having a sponsorship program in your workplace won't turn white people into true allies.

When I'm told about a formal sponsorship program in a company, I always ask about the results. I want to know where the people who are being sponsored are in the organization. What level did they start at and where are they today? I am always curious about how such programs influence outcomes for Black women.

As you may surmise, I am not a strong proponent of formal sponsorship programs unless organizations are prepared to link such programs to results. For a sponsorship program to lead to visible results in the careers of Black women, both the organization overall and the individual leaders who agree to be sponsors need to be held accountable.

Even when your organization says that it is committed to your success as a Black woman, do the homework to learn which people in positions of leadership and authority are viewed in your organization as potential sponsors. Then make sure that you are being transparent about your intentions and goals with those who can help you and that they are also clear with you. When you are building relationships and starting with a less formal relationship of mentorship, make sure that they are sponsorship material or can connect with the right peers at the right time in order to position you for advancement.

Where Do I Start?

Some of you may thinking, "This all sounds great, but where do I start?" You may still be in a phase where you are building relationships with mentors or you may be at an even earlier stage and have not built a direct connection with anyone yet. Your journey toward establishing a formal sponsorship connection should start with the tactics discussed in chapter six, reaching out to professionals and cultivating a network. Sponsorship is an escalation of the professional connections you can make by requesting meetings with people to learn from them.

While it is up to you to initiate and cultivate professional relationships, ultimately it is the sponsor who will make the decision to sponsor you, not the other way around, so it is necessary to prepare and position yourself in a way that will impress potential sponsors. Forming relationships with potential sponsors won't be easy. It will be an uphill battle, despite what the countless five-hundred-word articles on this topic may imply. Not everyone you reach out to will respond, someone you've built a relationship with may suddenly leave the organization, you might change your career goals and have to start building relationships from the ground up in a new industry. As I've emphasized, professional relationships take time, preparation, and energy. But they are worth every minute of it.

When you are pursuing a connection with the end goal of sponsorship, be explicit about the relationship you ultimately want. You can start by pursuing mentorship, but let them know that you hope that they will eventually sponsor you. Select someone that you know the organization sees as someone with the ability to be a sponsor. Don't waste your time cultivating a relationship with someone who can't help you achieve the career advancement outcomes you want. To identify the correct potential, you will need to do research that goes much deeper than learning a person's job title and responsibilities.

When you are very junior in your career and don't have many connections, you may have to start with someone who has a small amount of power and influence. Regardless of where you start with your search, always keep your career goals in mind. I was fortunate to have many big players sponsor me, but I had to work up to those relationships. Take the time to figure out who can help you reach the sponsorship relationship that you are looking for. Such work often starts with ensuring the right support even if you must start at the level of your peers. Know that sponsorship, even by a minor player, counts tremendously as it allows you to build toward more powerful sponsorship relationships.

For example, if you would like a sponsor who has global responsibility in your organization or a senior leadership role but are only able to attract a sponsor who has a smaller role, you can always ask them to help you form connections with more senior people once you've built a relationship of trust. He or she will understand your desire for a wider network of sponsors if you approach this in a professional manner. More than likely, they will help you to get to that next level and forge

relationships with other sponsors whose experience and position align more closely with your ultimate career goals.

This is not about climbing from one leader to the next. It's
important to secure the support of many people in your organization, and a network of sponsors can help you do that. Here
is where the reciprocity in the sponsorship role comes into play.
A sponsor can use their political capital to help you achieve
your goals and in return, you can help them with the resources
you have. Be clear about what you can offer the people who
support you (for example, your social capital, support for their
initiatives, or free lines of communication between the two of
you). If you don't take the time to explore and understand what
you bring to a sponsoring relationship, you run the risk of not
being able to gain the support of powerful people. Mentoring
and sponsoring are not one-way relationships.

A Tale of Two Sponsors

When Sam asked his question about who would be willing to
pound on the table for me, I had two potential sponsors in my
network, Lee and Robin. The dimensions of my relationships
with these two executives demonstrate many of the benefits
you should be looking for from a sponsor.

Both Lee and Robin had leadership positions and real
authority. They sat at a lot of tables where decisions about the
business and promotions were made. When they spoke, power
brokers in the company listened.

Lee had brought me into the organization. I could call on him
when I needed help, and he shared his perspective on difficult
situations when I needed it. He had seen me in action and knew
how I conducted myself as a leader and he often gave me feedback

after meetings he and I had attended. As a major player, he sat in the room when senior leadership spoke about me. I knew that Lee spoke up for me when I was not present. He openly supported me and my work. He always let me know what he said about me to others, especially in formal situations, and he shared what others had said about me. His approach to sponsorship was very hands on. I trusted him and his advice without question.

Robin had even broader influence than Lee. She was a major player on the business side and had a great deal of financial responsibility in our organization. Although Robin clearly had power, her name hadn't come to my mind immediately as a potential sponsor. She didn't see me in action every day, but I knew she spoke up for me in meetings. I made sure that she knew what I was doing through quarterly meetings with her. She had enough power to make decisions about my career with or without the support of others. Robin had broad reach within the organization and contacts with other leaders around the world. Even though she did not see me often, she had put me on projects and initiatives that had allowed the entire organization to see me in action and understand my contribution as a leader. The organization viewed her as a sponsor for me, as I learned from people I worked with. Ultimately, she and I came to refer to our relationship as one of sponsorship, both publicly and privately.

Together, these two sponsors provided valuable resources. Lee gave me insights and advice drawn from his long experience with the company. He frequently saw me in action and gave me feedback that helped me refine my style as a leader. Robin had the power to position me to be visible to everyone in the company and had a deep network of people around the world who could help me if need be.

What Makes a Good Sponsor?

First, a sponsor needs to be a good match for you and your goals. You must be able to help them and they must be in a position that is related to where you want to go in terms of department, level, function, or type of role. Look for things like similar educational backgrounds, people who are in your department, anyone whose work overlaps with yours, or someone who does the same functional job but at different levels. Your sponsor also needs to be a good fit in the eyes of the organization's leadership and those who will be assessing you for advancement potential.

It was clear that when Sam asked me who would pound their fist on the table for me, he was asking a much bigger question. He was speaking about power. Who was powerful enough in the organization to sponsor me? Both Lee and Robin were below him in the hierarchy of our organization. Were they powerful enough to support and influence Sam, one of the most powerful leaders at the company? The fact that someone sponsors you doesn't necessarily mean that they are the *right* sponsor for you. Sam wanted to compare my sponsors to his professional standard so he could decide if I was worthy of his support.

The most important criterion for a sponsor and the question you have to answer about each person you consider pursuing is not whether they are willing to sponsor you, although that question is important. What you need to evaluate is whether the organization sees the person you're considering as your sponsor as a powerful advocate. Do leaders at higher levels than your potential sponsor(s) view them as people with authority and influence?

Not all of the leaders who sit at the table have the same voice in the organization. This was one of the main differences between my two sponsors. Although Lee was less senior than Robin, his opinions carried a lot of weight. The organization listened to Lee more seriously than they did when Robin spoke. When you're considering a person as your sponsor, ask yourself who listens to them, who goes to them for help or advice regarding big projects, who talks about them in your organization and what do they say. Obviously an ideal sponsor should be more powerful than you, but they don't have to be the most powerful person in your organization. Just make sure you know how they are viewed within the company.

Once you get that first sponsor, you need to keep looking for other people who can become sponsors. Robin, who was more senior, became my first sponsor, but Lee was also critical to my success. The informal influence Lee had was ultimately just as powerful as Robin's more formal power. Building relationships with sponsors is a long-term project. Be strategic and know that your progress will not necessarily be linear.

In sum:

1. Your sponsor has to be more powerful than you, but they don't have to be the most powerful person in your organization or even in your division or function. You can start with people just a few levels ahead of you and work your way up.

2. Don't forget to consider informal power. People who are lower on the organizational chart can be effective sponsors if they are a right fit. For example, if you are in finance, but want to move into operations, the best sponsor is not

going to be the head of operations. The better choice may be someone in operations who works closely with you in your current department. Despite not being the leader, if this person is trusted in their own department, they can still be a powerful advocate for you. They know you, your work, and they understand how to position your strengths in finance so that those in operations will recognize the value you can bring to this other department.

3. Your sponsor has to be powerful enough that their advocacy on your behalf will be meaningful. Always be sure to observe how effective someone is before you pursue sponsorship. You need to form relationships with people whose perspective and judgment are taken seriously.

There Are Those Who Will Decline

Many people erroneously assume that because we are all human, we have similar experiences regardless of our race, ethnicity, gender, or background. This belief translates to an assumption that anyone higher than you in the organizational chart would qualify as a good sponsor. The reality is that some people don't want the role of mentor or sponsor. For example, for many reasons, some women and women of color don't want to support others, much less sponsor them.

My advice is to not worry about them or what they think. When you realize that someone isn't willing to mentor or sponsor, don't spend any time trying to understand what is going on with them or their reasons for their decision. That is not your work or mission. Advancing your career is what should be important to you and where you should expend your precious energy. Black women have enough challenges. The long-term goal is to get enough of us in the room at the right level to change this over time.

What If Your Sponsor Leaves the Organization?

You always want to have more than one sponsor who advocates for and supports you in your organization. When you have only one sponsor and they leave the organization, you no longer have an advocate at work. To avoid this, you need more than one leader in your corner speaking about you throughout your organization. I call this concept of having broad organizational support organizational advocacy.

Sometimes when a sponsor leaves an organization, the people they sponsored also leave. That is one of the risks of a sponsorship relationship. I had one sponsor who went on to another company. I did not learn that he had left until the announcement was published. He had to keep his plans confidential until the move was official. I did keep in contact with him and we remained part of each other's broader professional networks. Fortunately, I had formed relationships with others who had begun to support me. I remember my colleagues asking me what I was going to do now that my sponsor was leaving. My answer was that I would continue doing what I had been doing. I wasn't leaving and I had no intention of following that sponsor because I had a solid career and a good professional trajectory on the horizon. I was going to stay put because my sponsor and I had worked hard to set me up for success. I did not want to waste that good work.

Making a Tough Decision

Data and research have shown that sponsorship is the path to the C-suite for Black women, full stop. Most often, white men are the individuals in C-suite positions who can provide sponsorship. They are the leaders who have the power in organizations, at both the C-suite level and at all levels below that. Many white men will sponsor and support Black women, but many won't.

I am also a realist. There is no shortage of Black women professionals who are qualified to lead, and there are many of us who aspire to reach leadership levels. Despite this, the systems are old and slow to change, and we are still fighting an uphill battle. We have to be intentional about ensuring that we are prepared, positioned, and sponsored. You need to be discussed in the human capital reviews of your company and slated to take on leadership and executive positions in your company's plans. You must be very intentional about achieving this goal for yourself. You must use the power of your voice to create the narrative about your expectations and take the necessary actions. The people who can position you in the talent pipeline are your sponsors.

If you aren't getting opportunities and don't have sponsors in your current organization, you need to make decisions about where you want your career to go. Determine what career you want to have and whether you are with an organization that can provide you with what you need to reach your long-term career goals. Can you obtain the sponsor you need to achieve your goals in the position you hold?

Making your own decisions sometimes that means leaving your company to seek an organization where you can get the sponsorship and support you need because they are ready for you to lead. Make sure that you are in an organization that shares your values about advancing Black women. If you value your career and professional advancement and your organization isn't moving within the time frame you have set, you know what you need to do.

Don't be hesitant or shy. Your mission is to obtain the professional success you deserve. One sponsor will not make or break your career success, nor one organization. Don't let one person or one organization get in the way of your career advancement.

CHAPTER EIGHT

Place Her on the Flip Chart Over There

" **S**o who knows her?" This question would come after someone's manager had presented them as talent to the organization.

A silence would come over the room as the woman's manager looked around anxiously while everyone appeared to be in deep thought and reflection. But they weren't thinking about the woman whose name had been mentioned or preparing what they would say about her. Their silence spoke volumes.

Then someone would inevitably say, "Let's place her over there," referring to a flip chart where the names of employees the power brokers in the room didn't know anything about were recorded.

The meeting was the organization's succession planning discussion. Strangely, although a great deal of preparation happened before this meeting, very little was known about it in the organization at large and by the people—the "talent"—who were the subjects of the meeting.

These meetings, some of which lasted hours, an entire day, or even several days, were high priority and required considerable time and effort. However, what was often missing from the meetings was accountability from the people making the decisions.

Often the only person who knew enough about someone to bring them forward was their manager. However, one person's advocacy usually wasn't adequate. More than one person in that meeting needed to agree that a person should be viewed as promotable. One sponsor is never enough. You need to have relationships with people who operate on multiple levels of your organization.

Organizational Advocacy and Power

Institutions benefit from systemic power that was built centuries ago, beginning with the industrial revolution and the advent of the modern corporation. These organizations and systems remain powerful today. They are revered by many and make money for their stockholders, for the market itself, and even sometimes for their employees. The power that these organizations wield in today's ever-evolving workplace is going nowhere. It is woven tightly within the fabric of an organization and our society and it simply won't change overnight.

However, an organization is only as powerful as its people, which means each individual and, ultimately, you. Making sure you provide something that the organization wants, and making sure they know this, will be key to getting them to advocate for you. The organization has something that you want as well, so you support them naturally through your employment, i.e., fulfilling the requirements of your job description. Beyond your employment, if what you want is to advance in your career to a position of leadership and authority, then you will need a whole network of relationships across the organization. You need to work to get the organization behind you during the good times and the bad ones.

Once you have established this larger network of relationships and a strong visible brand and reputation, the relationship between you and your organization won't be about delivery alone. Once you have reached that stage in the relationship with your organization, you will share in their power. When those who are genuine representatives of the organization advocate for you, their support takes on the weight of the whole organization as an entity. This is the power you will gain from having what I call organizational advocacy.

You Don't Want to Be on the Flip Chart

When that silence would fall over the succession planning meeting, there was little a manager could do. When no one said anything to support the person a manager was presenting, the person would usually become just as quiet as the others in the room. They had their own career to protect.

The only exception to this protocol was if the person presenting the talent was the most senior person in the room or had the most power. If such a leader brought up a name that was unfamiliar, everyone would agree with their assessment. However, that rarely happened. Powerful leaders don't often bring up names of people that others in the room don't already know something about.

When that silence would fall, in order to keep the meeting moving, the name would go on a list titled "Get to Know Better." In my mind, I labeled this list "No Intention to Get to Know

Better." Often there was no plan or process for doing something with the names on the list. No one took responsibility for that list of names. What was even worse was that the people whose names were on the list usually never found out that powerful people in the organization didn't know them.

What manager is going to go back to their direct report and say, "I bought up your name during the talent review meeting, but no one knew you." This would especially not happen if the direct report was a woman and definitely not if she was a Black woman with a white manager.

In my role in HR, it was often left up to me to approach such an employee. It wasn't required, but I often felt a sense of responsibility because I wondered how many lists I was on that I didn't know about. So I often encouraged a leader to inform their direct report what had happened or decided to tell the individual myself that they needed to have a conversation with their manager about their career, especially if that person was a member of a marginalized group. I always did so for Black women because so few of us even got as far as that list.

These succession planning discussions often determined the future of someone's career. It was only the first step for some-one's manager to feel they were worthy of consideration at these meetings. Although the leader presenting the individual would know what that person had accomplished, what they wanted from their career, and what the next step for them would ide-ally be, one advocate in the room was never enough.

When someone's name was placed on the flip chart, it wasn't because they necessarily had a bad reputation. They may be con-sidered a good worker, and they may even have had a reputation for good work that spanned divisions, departments, and levels. Names went on that flip chart because support for that person was not support for them *as a future leader*. It is not enough to have a reputation for good work. It is necessary to have a reputation for leadership potential across a broader network.

Do you have that kind of support in your organization? You need to look beyond your function or your department. You should be building your brand beyond the people you work with you directly. Leaders who make decisions about your future could be hearing someone else's perspective about you and they will weigh that information as heavily as what they hear from your manager and your colleagues. Does everyone share a vision of you as someone with leadership potential? You need a network of supporters throughout your organization that supports you and can envision you advancing in your career. That group needs to go beyond your manager and your sponsors.

Even if the most powerful person in your company is one of your sponsors, you need supporters throughout your organization. Powerful people need to see that others are also advocating for you. And I'm not just talking about the big meetings like succession planning reviews or talent discussions. There are also many individuals who may not be in the room but who serve as influencers. You also need to know who they are and how they can help you. We need a team. People are discussed all the time in organizations. Any conversation that is relevant to the work you do or the work you would like to do is a time when the support of people in leadership positions can manifest itself—or not.

It is important to understand how to build that support in your organization. You want others to see you in action regularly. It is also important to understand your organization's talent review processes, where you fit in the company's plans, and the roles of the people in the room during important meetings.

You need to ask people how such meetings work in your company. Before a meeting that has an agenda related to your work or work you would like to do, find out whether you will be discussed. After the meeting, ask someone you trust what was said. You need to take the initiative to learn these things. Leaving it up to someone else, even your manager, to approach you to share the outcome of a meeting usually will mean that you won't know what happened.

Relying on your immediate manager or leader to support you in important meetings isn't adequate. You have to continually build and maintain organizational advocacy by nurturing relationships with people who can advocate for you. Your advocates need to know specific details about you and your work at any given time.

When Your Name Doesn't Even Make It into the Room

But what if your name isn't even mentioned, even though it's placed on the flip chart? This has nothing to do with your performance. It may be outstanding. You may have just led a big project that saved the company thousands of dollars. Your manager might personally think you could take over the company someday. If only our work translated into promotions that directly!

The issue is that many Black professional women do not advance far enough in their company to become known. Many people in power do not think that Black women have the ability to become leaders or executives. As a result, Black women are often positioned below the threshold where power players start to consider people for leadership roles. This means that their managers are also low on the organizational chart. So even when Black women's managers are in the succession planning meetings, they aren't powerful enough to advocate for the Black women who report to them.

I was fortunate to discover this early in my career when I was still quite junior. Although I was not often in the rooms where the talent was discussed, I helped my boss prepare for such meetings. I knew who would be in the room because I was responsible for preparing packets of information for each attendee. It dawned on me that these were the individuals who had power in the company because they were the ones who made the decisions. Because my role was in human resources, I also knew who they selected, who they considered for selection, and who wasn't even considered.

Armed with my new insights, I took the opportunity to discuss my own performance and potential with my manager. I also made sure that his manager knew about me and my work. My goal was to ensure that more than one person knew about me as a person, not just about the specific deliverables and responsibilities of my job. I knew that talent reviews and succession planning were about much more than what people had accomplished.

I often ask Black women whether they know how the talent or succession planning processes work at their company or who the key players are in such discussions. Many can't tell me or they tell me what the organization has written about the process, which is usually a brief overview that says very little about how it really works. You need to learn the details of how your company conducts talent reviews. When these meetings are held, your relationship with your immediate manager or leader won't be enough. You will need to have people throughout the organization who know who you are, regardless of where you are in the company.

As I became more senior and became one of the decision makers in those meetings, I saw that the names on the talent and succession charts were mostly the names of people who didn't look like me. This wasn't because there weren't Black women in the organizations I worked for. They most certainly were there. It wasn't a pipeline issue, the excuse that so many companies give for the absence of Black women at the senior and executive levels.

The issue was that we were so buried in the organization that our names never made it to the talent or succession planning processes. Many organizations only want to look for candidates for promotion above a certain level. Because of that, the leaders who sit in talent and succession planning reviews never get to know who we are. Our names never come up.

No One Is Going to Do It for You

Once I knew who would be in the room as I prepared for many talent reviews and succession planning sessions, I made sure that those decision makers knew who I was. I shared my plans for my career and what I wanted to do. I didn't have all of the details, but I refined my thinking as I grew my career. As I became more senior, I became clearer. I engaged people in my success beyond my mentors, my sponsors, and my manager or their manager.

You will always need to make sure that the right people have the right point of view about you, no matter what level you are and even if those people don't know you that well. When individuals other than your manager know about you, your work, and your ability to contribute at an even higher level, you will be better positioned for success in your career. Look outside your function for opportunities to contribute that are related to the current work you are doing. Pay attention to the world outside your immediate bubble, to the company's long-term strategic goals. Actively integrate those goals into your everyday work. Consider your own personal development in the context of the goals and priorities of your organization.

I always asked myself if there were people who needed to know about my work beyond my manager. I had the opportunity to connect with leaders who I knew would be in the room where the organization's talent would be discussed because I prepared information for them. I'm sure all of us do some form of this in our current jobs. Consider what you know about other people's job functions. Even if you are at the very beginning of your career, do you schedule meetings? Do you support other staff and take or write up notes? You almost certainly know more about who does what than you might initially realize.

Additionally, recognize that the important discussions don't always happen during the time your company designates for their succession planning review. Individuals and talent are discussed all the time in many meetings and at various levels. This is why it is important to build your reputation holistically; so many people in many departments know you and will be able to discuss your potential when these more spontaneous discussions happen. Though informal, these conversations can have just as much of an impact on your future.

In my experience, Black women don't make it into the room because they are waiting for someone to acknowledge them. Don't wait for permission to learn what you need to know. Opportunities come from many different people in positions of influence. Making sure those people know what you need them to know about you requires extra work, but career advancement and professional success isn't easy.

Don't let those in the room place you on a flip chart or ignore you because you are deep in your organization. As Black professional women, we can't wait for the power players to recognize us or our hard work. Our colleagues, especially white men, often speak up about their achievements. That may be uncomfortable to us, but it's necessary, as I learned the hard way. I believed that my work stood on its own and was always hopeful that that would translate to strong support for me in my company. Well, it didn't. I was labeled as a hard worker who was not strategic.

If you are relying on a few people to advocate for you or position you for success, you may be setting yourself up for disappointment. Gather the support you need from mentors, sponsors, allies, and advocates throughout the organization. This will create a broader consensus about your leadership potential.

One day it may be that our work and our accomplishments will stand for themselves, and not depend on subjective opinion. But until things change in the workplace, you will need to make sure that you have enough of the right people to speak on your behalf. Start lining them up if you haven't begun doing so already. Trust me, they will become invaluable to you.

CHAPTER NINE

At the Table, but Not Really

E xclusion is a powerful word. If you are a Black professional woman, the word is not new to you.

Exclusion can be exhausting, demoralizing, and hurtful. At a basic level, it means being left out. In the workplace, exclusion is characterized by a lack of relationships.

In today's workplace, exclusion is often covert. You will probably never be openly attacked in the workplace when others can see what is happening. You probably will never be openly told that you can't be a part of something in your organization or that you do not belong. This is not to say that these things never happen. I am simply saying that organizations and the people who work in them are a little savvier than they used to be. We've all experienced it, whether it's our manager or peers, who take actions which appear to be inclusive but in reality exclude people.

Have you ever been omitted from an email distribution that you should have been copied on? Have you ever been told that you are not needed at the meeting but will be brought up to speed later? I have always thought to myself, "Why bring me up to speed? I don't need a filtered version of something that I am a part of." This has happened to me when I had a key role, and even worse, on projects I was accountable for. No matter what level you reach, you can still be excluded. It is important to deal with exclusionary behavior when you suspect it is happening, because it is likely to get worse if you wait to address it.

Exclusion Is Powerful

Exclusion is power gone bad.

You may be invited into the room, but not included in the conversation. People in positions of power have the ability to exclude. But exclusion is not a behavior that is unique to people who lead—if it were only that simple. Everyone and every part of an institution can contribute to exclusion—managers, employees, systems, routines, and processes. Exclusion is not a behavior unique to those who lead only. If it were only that easy.

The deliberate exclusion that your peers participate in can be more insidious than the exclusion you experience from your direct manager or from people higher up the ladder. The behavior can be as simple as a project team that doesn't loop you in or a group that assigns you a task that won't do anything for your career or your reputation. They may even be less competent or capable than you. It is a painful experience, but there will always be folks like this and you will have to work with them anyway.

The question becomes how to handle the situation if you are being excluded. How can you succeed despite exclusion?

The first step in fighting back when individuals are intentionally blocking your success is to turn to your relationships with people who support you. When people intentionally choose not to invite you in, when they don't share the information you need to accomplish your goals or help prepare you or position you to succeed, you need people in your corner who *are* inviting you in and who will fight for you when someone else tries to push you out. These people can become the guardrails for you. They can ensure that you avoid a situation where you might be excluded and they can work to influence situations where you need to be included. They can help you respond to exclusion and they can help you manage the barriers because they are often a part of circle of power themselves. Insiders are often your best resource when you are fighting exclusion at work.

The workplace is a microcosm of the world at large. Those who work within a company often represent how individuals act and act in society. The workplace only represents one specific situation where exclusionary behaviors occur. Certain individuals are allowed, within systems and structures, to hide their actions and true beliefs. Unfortunately, those bad actors who practice exclusion in the workplace do this more covertly than overtly, which we often see in society as well. If this were not the case for Black women in the workplace, there would be no need for this book.

I have identified four major strategies for combatting exclusion in the workplace. They are not easy or quick, and they require you to be proactive and willing to grow. But they are powerful and necessary for you as a Black woman building your career.

Never Trust and Always Verify

I had been given feedback for the umpteenth time that I needed to speak up because I was "too quiet" in meetings. People needed to hear my voice and my perspectives were important—or so I was told. I was encouraged to take risks. My manager, Angelica, told me that the only way I would be seen as a future leader was to share my thoughts, whether they were right or wrong. I took this advice to heart and it backfired on me.

I vividly recall sitting next to Angelica to show solidarity. We were in a contentious meeting and after the feedback I had been given about speaking up, I thought to myself, "I guess I need to take the lead." I would do what I thought my manager expected of me and I assumed that she would be assessing my ability to do this.

The discussion was heated, tempers were running high, and people were speaking over each other to the point where I recall raising my hand in order to be acknowledged. During the discussion, we reached an impasse. The talking stopped, and I used the opportunity to speak up to offer a recommendation. My hope was that people in the room would listen to me and we could reach a temporary solution. Instead, the reaction to my comment was immediate and unquestionably hostile.

Later, Angelica accused me of causing the walkout because I had spoken up when I should have just listened. She said that she never told me to speak up *during* the meeting. She told me that her message to me had been that although I should speak up, it was important to ensure that I picked the right time. She said that I had picked the wrong time. And to make matters worse, she claimed that I should have understood from the dynamics in the room that it wasn't the time for me to speak. The result of this interaction was that I was excluded from all subsequent meetings with this group.

I was certain that I had understood the direction my manager had given me, and I recognized that her backpedaling about knowing when to speak up was a rather thin attempt to regain control and avoid responsibility. But I learned a valuable lesson.

Never trust and always verify.

Always clearly understand the specific actions someone wants you to take and the details associated with them when it relates to your performance and your career development. There was no question that my manager had been referring to the meeting we were preparing to have with this group when she told me to speak up. She had even brought up a previous meeting with the same group as an example of a time when she had wanted me to speak up. She had pointed to the second meeting as an opportunity where she expected me to do so.

It seemed clear enough, but obviously it was not. The lesson I learned was to always get very specific information about what was expected of me and then to confirm that I understood the instructions accurately. Before the second meeting, I should have gone to her to play out scenarios and get clarity about our specific roles in the meeting. I should have asked my manager to clearly communicate the expected outcome of the meeting.

In a subsequent meeting, Angelica did not accept any accountability and blamed me for the resulting lack of resolution. Of course I wasn't happy about this and I decided to not let it happen again.

Never Rely On One Source of Support

Another way to verify is to seek out people you have relationships with to get other perspectives in a situation like this. In this case, I decided to verify with others whether Angelica's view of me as too quiet was a perspective others shared. I felt that was an example of something bigger that I needed to find out about the organization.

I was often not the first or second person in a meeting to speak up. I detested when people who had nothing to say spoke up. I called them "air-takers." As I had been trained to do growing up, I often listened before I spoke. But when I spoke it had meaning, and I thought that was more important than just speaking up with little to share. However, I realized that it was possible that others in the organization had the same view of me as my manager and that I needed to know whether that was the case.

It dawned on me that my manager had the power not only to exclude me but also to say something about me that was not entirely accurate to other people in the organization. Your manager should not be the only one who has a point of view about you. If your manager is the only person who is helping you navigate your career, you run the risk of being kept hidden from others in the organization. Most important, if your manager is your only advocate, your manager's narrative about you becomes the narrative other people know about you. The organization will know you only through your manager's voice.

Seeking feedback from allies about how your actions are perceived is a powerful strategy because it works for you on both fronts: it can help you out of a situation where you are being excluded, but it can also help you build the positive relationships that form the foundation of advocacy across an organization. I wasn't at any leadership table at this juncture in my career and I didn't have much power in my company, but what I learned from this experience was invaluable. This experience helped me understand how to proceed once I was sitting at the table.

When your direct manager isn't supporting you, you often have to go to others who are more powerful than your manager.

Seek Out Truth-Telling Relationships

After Angelica's feedback, I went to Beth, a mentor I trusted. Beth wasn't a leader in the organization, but I could count on her to tell me the truth. She knew the organization very well and I had watched her navigate through many situations.

Always make sure that you have someone in your corner who is willing to tell you the truth, no matter how tough it is, and who can help you understand what the truth means to you. I call these people my truth tellers and "org decoders." Beth verified that people often described me as smart but quiet. Many had noticed my "quiet approach," as it was termed. Beth told me that being quiet or waiting for the right time to have something to say could hurt my career. She explained that speaking early in a meeting mattered to the company's leaders. The people who received meaningful assignments or promotions in the organization were the ones who were outspoken and always shared a point of view early on even if it wasn't 100 percent accurate.

Beth said that my "quiet approach" was demonstrating to the company that I might not be willing to take risks if it meant failing. The company valued risk taking highly. To the people who were watching me, being quiet meant being cautious. That was how I was starting to be known as in the company.

The brand I thought I had was not the brand the organization saw. More important, it wasn't a brand the organization valued or sought in the people it deemed to have leadership potential. I never saw myself as being cautious or quiet, but a person's perception is their reality. In the end, I was glad that my manager had said what she did about me and even that she had blamed me for the outcome of that meeting. That experience inspired me to get other opinions and learn what was important to the organization. I learned what was at risk if I continued to go down a path the organization didn't value.

You need to know and understand what is getting in the way of your success. This is what I say to anyone who is working to move a career forward or overcome obstacles. Some of the perceptions about you can be adjusted and some can't. The views about you that you can't change are the ones that are embedded in a person or in the entire organization and will never change. These issues are part of the institution's and even society's fabric and are often too big for you to overcome.

Once you have information about why or how you're being excluded, you need to decide whether you can tolerate what is happening to you. Can you adjust to it or should you choose not to? Your answer to that question may mean that you need to leave the organization, and that's OK. You should never stick around in an environment that is not meeting your career expectations. Such a work environment will only become unhealthy for you over time. No one should tough it out unless they have a reasonable hope that a situation will pay off for them in the near future.

Sometimes we, as Black women, are hopeful that something will become better for us if we stick it out and exhaust all avenues in our company. But if you're not completely confident that your contribution will lead to career success, move on. One company will not define you. Each organization I left taught me something valuable about my career.

The meeting with Angelica and the employees was a catalyst for me to learn something about my company's culture that could only have become a bigger problem in my career. The incident bothered me enough to propel me but to look beyond that meeting and ask someone I trusted to help me understand what was at risk for me in that company. I chose not to let one person exclude me from being successful.

Keep Others Accountable

After I received the feedback from Beth, I had another conversation with Angelica. My goal was to let her know that I clearly understood the feedback I had received. I wanted to know exactly what I should have done differently. I also wanted to know how we would proceed as a manager and a direct report. In short, I wanted to hold her accountable.

My unyielding rule today is never let your manager—or anyone—give you feedback without holding them accountable for their words. Even though the situation may be about an action you need to take or a behavior you need to change, make sure that they own their feedback. It took a lot of courage for me to go beyond accepting what my manager was telling me. I decided that my manager needed to help me.

Documentation is your friend, especially when accountability is an issue. After a conversation like the second one I had with Angelica, write a follow-up email to your manager documenting the agreements and advice they gave you. Send it to them within a day of the conversation, ideally the same day, and ask if the email accurately reflects what you talked about, the expectations they set for you, and the plans you made for moving forward. If they make any suggestions or corrections, reply in the affirmative. Keep this email and all of their responding emails. Refer to them in subsequent conversations. Curiosity is your friend. Should their feedback in the future deviate from what you have discussed, don't accuse them of anything, simply forward them the emails you saved, point out how you followed their advice, and ask what you should have done differently.

Although the things Angelica accused me of weren't accurate and didn't match what she had told me to do before the meeting, I still needed to enroll her in my overall success. I chose not to walk away in silence but to instead get advice and help. Always take the initiative to make decisions for yourself instead of letting them be made for you. If I had remained silent after Angelica's interactions with me, I would have been letting my manager make my career decisions for me.

I chose to play for something bigger. Yes, I felt excluded and a little embarrassed—well, a lot. But I chose to look past it as the incident became less significant to me than the information I learned from it. I determined that I needed to focus on my career and let others, including my manager, see my work.

Exclusion can show up in many ways at work. It can manifest in a feeling that you always need to watch out and be suspicious or that you are being told that your understanding of something is in your imagination (gaslighting at its best) or that you're too sensitive. Being told that you are trying to put a racial or gender slant on how you're being treated is insulting. I've had those conversations. Against these obstacles, it is no wonder that Black women face such challenges in their efforts to reach levels of power in their careers.

Before you can get a seat at the table, you have to get access to the room where the table is. Once you have made it into the room, then you can work on achieving that seat, which is a feat unto itself. Then the work becomes about ensuring that you remain at the table with people in positions of leadership and authority. But don't forget your peers and those below you. There is no honorary acceptance or lifelong membership, ever. Be aware that nothing is promised and that a seat at the table is never guaranteed.

Even after you have successfully made it to the highest levels at your organization, you will face an ongoing fight not to be excluded. The thing that will change as you rise in your career is that the risk of being excluded becomes higher and more covert. For those that have achieved success as a Black woman at work, you come to find the harsh reality is that it becomes even harder to succeed and stay in those upper echelons.

CHAPTER TEN

Bullied, Backstabbed, and Boxed In

I never felt that I couldn't do my job. I always felt that I could do anything or overcome any obstacle that was put in front of me at work. The term "imposter syndrome" was never in my vocabulary or my thinking. What was in my mind was that I would achieve "in spite of" and that if something got in my way, I would handle it. Usually by the time I did get a job, I'd already been doing it.

Sound familiar? Being overeducated, overqualified, and overly ready is just who we are and what we do. Very early on in my career, I received a "promotion" that I had been waiting for, was clearly prepared for, and was capable of taking on, or so I thought. As relationships are critical to your success, when they go wrong, they can also be the biggest roadblocks you will face in your career.

What I thought was going to be an awesome opportunity that would position me for a more senior role turned out to be one of the worst jobs I've ever had. But it was also one of the important learning experiences that prepared me to reach the level of a global vice-president at age 38.

I can see this executive, Aaron, even today in my mind, as I stood in his office door. I had asked for a meeting after hearing that he didn't think I had a future at the company. I wanted to know why he thought that and what I could do to improve. Instead of giving me constructive feedback, I was met with condescension, and he minimized my concerns. For the first time in my life, tears poured down my face in full view of my boss and my whole office.

I had never cried in a workplace before, but on that day I was broken. All the confidence I had built and all the positive feedback I had received over the years of my career disappeared in that moment. With barely an indifferent glance in my direction, he dismissed me. Aaron refused to make eye contact with me and stared at his computer as I walked back to my office.

As I look back, I now recognize the red flags in Aaron's behavior and I understand that the problem was not me. This leader was a professional bully and he was bullying me.

Here are a few of his behaviors that I now recognize as bullying:

1. It had become what seemed like Aaron's standard practice to complain about me. This was done not only behind closed doors but also in public situations such as business meetings with our entire team.

2. He was usually the most senior person in the room, and no one was willing to stand up to him because he had the power to destroy people's careers. He didn't spare me or any of the others on the team his scathing, public criticism. Everyone knew this leader's wrath.

3. Aaron was proud of his ability to assess talent with an "up or out" mind-set. Mercy was rare. His idea of having mercy on me was a condescending comment that "I'd make it through this."

4. He could never tell me exactly what I had done wrong or what he didn't like about my work. Eventually I stopped asking. I didn't want to give him ammunition to build a case that he'd given me feedback that I wasn't doing anything about. I had seen him use that tactic before and I was determined to avoid it.

The moment he dismissed me from that meeting, I knew it was time to get out of his department. It was clear that no amount of talking, seeking clarity, or asking for additional feedback would change his opinion of me. When you recognize these behaviors in a manager or superior, know that the problem is not you—it's them. This is when you need to turn to your network and start planning your exit, either to another department or to a different company.

What Are Professional Bullies?

Workplace bullies are people who intimidate others based on their place in the hierarchy. They create hostile work situations. They prey on those who have less power than they do. They use their power coercively. This is what I experienced, and to this day, I still don't know why. It's rare to uncover a bully's motivations, and it's largely a waste of your time to try. Just know that it has nothing to do with you. It is always something within them that motivates their behavior.

When you are faced with this sort of toxic workplace relationship, there will be times when you need to ask for help and there will be times when you need to just get out. Getting out doesn't necessarily mean leaving your company. If that is necessary, then take action and do it. You may have the opportunity to grow your career in a company you like working for. If you have one roadblock that you feel that you can work around, then think creatively about what you might do within the organization, taking into consideration your career, your health, and your sanity.

I wasn't ready to give up, as that just isn't in my nature. I had worked exceptionally hard to get to places where I was the only Black person, not just at work but often in the entire community. I had worked long hours, doing the work of more than one person. I had made up my mind that I had given my company a lot of myself, both professionally and personally. I had invested in the company. I had delivered beyond their expectations in all of the positions I had had. I had the performance evaluations to prove this and the feedback to support this. I expected a return on my investment.

Armor against Bullies

The belief you have in your ability to succeed in the workplace as a Black woman is power in itself. That confidence can be taken away from you only if you let it. But that doesn't mean that there won't be times when someone tries to take it from you.

There will be times when all you have worked for and believe to be true about yourself as a professional and all the positive feedback the organization has communicated to you will be challenged. All of us have had an experience when a coworker has tried to erode our belief in our ability to be successful. Frequently this happens for no apparent reason.

These individuals may have more power than you, either formal power or informal. They may also have power equal to you. The level doesn't matter. What does matter is their intentions. Their goal is to shake your confidence, but they are often also after your reputation. They will try to engage others in their attempt to sabotage your professional success.

To protect the confidence that you have painstakingly built, it is critical to mobilize the help of people you have partnered with. People who are in positions of power in your company or even your peers will become key resources for helping you navigate through a situation with a workplace bully. When the bully tries to engage others to damage your position, having your own network of relationships is the best armor you can have.

Sometimes these allies will be able to help you before you are aware that you need help. They may be able to see something happening that you don't have information about. It is crucially important to surround yourself with people who support you, who believe in you and your professional ability. If you have nurtured those relationships and built up your political capital with them during the good times, you will be able to count on them during the bad times.

When you are dealing with a bully, your power lies in knowing when to call in your allies to help you. They are the ones that will help you navigate a bad situation or relationship. Be confident in yourself and in their ability to help you.

Leveraging Adversity for a Bigger Win down the Road

I learned several very painful lessons from this episode in my career, but they have ultimately given me some of the most powerful tools in my arsenal.

Lesson One. When you are offered the opportunity to take on a project that is in deep trouble, even if someone claims that they are offering you the opportunity to be the hero, be careful. Ask yourself, "Why are they putting me in front of a train wreck?" The confrontation I described above came about because I was in HR and the company had offered me the opportunity to "fix" Aaron's management skills. Individuals don't change, especially if they are not required to do so and especially when they are rewarded for their work instead of for how they treat their team, their peers, and their subordinates. Just because the organization believes you are the one who can right a capsized boat doesn't mean that you will succeed. It's more than likely that the boat will sink no matter what you do. The assignment I was given to fix Aaron's management style was doomed from the beginning and it was only a matter of time before I became his target.

Lesson Two. Never rely on only one relationship or one manager to champion your career. I had been interacting with Aaron as a potential sponsor. I was working to convince him that I was a future star in the organization. I assumed that his opinion of me carried so much weight with power players that I hadn't involve others in my career. I felt that he was the only one I needed for my success. This was a poor assumption. It was precisely because I was relying solely on him to speak up for my work that he was able to bully me. I had allowed him to make it difficult for me to move ahead; he had boxed me in. My career success was totally reliant on him.

Lesson Three. Don't waste your energy trying to make things work with a bully. Use your energy to focus on building positive relationships with others. When you talk to these allies, instead of complaining about the negative relationship with the bully, focus on yourself by asking them for feedback and take every opportunity to let them see you in action. Your good work will pay off.

Lesson Four. The saying goes, "If you're going through hell, then keep going." My addition to this statement is, "Yes, but have a plan, because it won't get any better." Always have a plan no matter what level you are in your organization or where you are in your career.

Lesson Five. Always know what you are willing to do and what you aren't willing to do. Only you can decide where those lines are. Although speaking to others about Aaron's behavior and calmly stating the facts to allow them to draw their own conclusions may sound like the obvious strategy, it wasn't that easy to do. I had to be prepared for the possibility that I would be blamed for the conflict.

Aaron was a much, much more powerful player than me. He delivered results and had a strong reputation. I believe that is why he was allowed to behave in such a manner; the organization reinforced his behavior by tolerating it. However, I went to leaders who shared my values. They respected me and I respected them. They had the power to make a change for me. Fortunately, I was able to move into another role and Aaron was demoted. The "bad marriage" ended.

When the Challenge Goes into Stealth Mode

When you become more senior, the opposition to you goes underground if someone doesn't like you or what you stand for. This kind of opposition can be more costly to you and more dangerous to your career. Later in my career, I encountered another bully who was even worse than Aaron. I was thankful that I had navigated through dealing with a bully early in my career. That experience prepared me for the bigger and more subtle bullying, the boxing in, and the sabotaging of confidence that often occurs in the workplace that no one likes to talk about.

This person, who I'll call Karen, was very passive-aggressive. While Aaron's bullying was overt and bold, Karen's actions were covert and her knife was so sharp, you didn't even feel it when she stabbed you in the back. Karen always agreed with me in public, said she supported my work, and praised me openly, but behind the scenes she spoke about me differently. The lessons I had learned early on about having others know about your work became crucial to my success and even to my job.

This is why it so important to pay attention to the subtle language people use and the subtle messages that people send about you, especially if you are a Black woman. Karen claimed to be my advocate, but in fact she was the opposite. Bias rarely manifests itself in direct feedback. Those who give you feedback will hide their bias under other "plausible" comments, because they don't want to be labeled discriminatory, to admit that they don't like you or that they are biased. You need to look at behavior to see someone's true colors.

The first bombshell came from a quick call I had as I was driving home from work. I was speaking to a colleague in leadership who I trusted without reservation because we had helped each other many times over the years. I had advocated for her to become a senior leader in my organization and she had supported me as well. She called to tell me that I needed to be careful about Karen. At a talent-planning meeting, Karen had said to her senior peers that I didn't "play nice" with others.

Fortunately, people in the room, including the leader who called me, had disagreed with her.

The next day, a meeting appeared on my calendar out of nowhere. It was with a leader in my organization who was someone I didn't know very well. I didn't know what the meeting was about but I accepted it, since we were the only people of color in the organization's leadership at that time.

After I accepted the mysterious meeting, I walked past the office of a colleague to get a cup of coffee. As I passed by, he summoned me into his office with some urgency and asked me to shut the door. I sat down at his conference table. He said a sentence that I will never forget: "Francine, you need to get out of here; we can no longer protect you."

By that time, I knew immediately what he was talking about. As he told me what had happened in the meeting the previous day, he said that my ears should have been burning. Karen had described me as an ineffective leader of my department. She had added that I had limited career potential and should not be given any opportunities to advance further. I listened in dismay, but I wasn't surprised after the warning I had received in the phone call.

This wasn't just about being bullied or boxed in or about the risk of being fired. This was about sabotaging my entire career. It is not an exaggeration to say that it was genuine backstabbing, since Karen had only expressed support for my work and future to me directly. The stakes were much higher than they had been in the conflict with Aaron. The higher you go up in an organization, the more sophisticated and covert the actions to harm you become and the more dangerous they become to your career. The potential harm to your reputation can spread to your entire industry.

But This Time I Was Prepared

Because I had learned my early lessons well, I had a very powerful network of relationships and allies. Two people who were senior executives had shared with me what they had heard and how they had defended me. They had warned me to take action. These were not gossipy individuals by any means, but they truly had my back. They remembered times when I had helped them and it was now their turn to help me.

My mystery meeting with a third executive happened later that week. He confirmed what the two other executives had told me. He said that he had supported me in the meeting because he knew of my work and its impact in the organization. He wasn't supporting me because we were both people of color. He was doing so because he was a savvy leader who understood the dynamics of the organization and could see Karen's motives for what they were.

Make sure that you build relationships with advocates outside your function or department as early as you can. Take action to make sure that others see your work. Look for an initiative outside your immediate team that you can participate in. Find one that has impact and will give you access and exposure to people who are leaders or peers of your manager who can speak on your behalf. Make sure that you are fulfilling your specific job responsibilities and the tasks your direct manager has assigned exceptionally well. This is always the baseline no matter what. It will be difficult for your allies to support you if you aren't delivering what you were hired to do.

Always ask yourself, "Who can I trust to support me in addition to my manager?" Know who these individuals are and take care to nurture those relationships. Always be aware that someone is watching you and what you do beyond your imme-diate manager and the people who are directly above you.

I didn't have this understanding earlier in my career when I faced a powerful executive who bullied me. But this time, instead of having to go to the organization for help, the organi-zation came to me in the form of three allies who rallied to help me. All the relationships I had built in the intervening years paid off tremendously.

It's never too early or too late to find people who are trust-worthy peers and leaders in your organization. These individu-als will reveal themselves to you if you pay close attention. The game you will have to play when someone is trying to block you includes players who don't want to see you succeed, but if you have relationships with many allies, you can succeed no matter what roadblock you encounter. The key is to surround yourself with people who share your goals for your career.

Because I had cultivated a dense network of allies, I got out of both situations with bullies and I got a promotion each time.

CHAPTER ELEVEN

Your
Soul
Is Not
for Sale

I've never left a job because I didn't like the job. (There are a few managers I can't say the same about.) I have, however, left jobs that represented opportunity but demanded a sacrifice I could not make. You will face moments in your career when who you are and what you stand for is something you're not willing to lose.

That may mean you'll have to make the decision to move on even when you did well, knowing that you and your career might not recover. But you will have held on to what you treasure and what is important to you personally. I came to the workplace with a solid foundation and a strong set of values. I would not have been able to survive and get as far as I did without the core values and purpose I brought to work every day.

When you are faced with a decision about whether to walk away from a job you love, your preparation for that moment will be the source of your resilience. Always be prepared to move forward, whether you are doing so for your own reasons or you are being pushed. Neither way is inherently bad. It's only bad when you have no course of action prepared and you're only responding to what you think might happen to you and your career. Don't let any organization make such an important career decision for you.

This is the time when all the actions you have taken to build your network—gaining support and advocacy from leaders in power, building implicit skills and learning the rules of your organization, calling on the support of your network—will start to work in your favor. Sometimes playing your best power hand means moving forward in your career and sometimes it means ensuring that you keep what you stand for intact and undamaged.

Your Relationship to Power

The relationship you have with power may bring thoughts and feelings of discomfort. This is especially true in the workplace. More than likely, your level of discomfort with power is even more pronounced when it is mentioned in the context of being successful in your career. This is because we have all heard about times about when power was abused and have sometimes been on the receiving end of power abuse. As a result, many of us feel conflicted about the issue of power, especially at work.

However, a successful career starts with your relationship with power. You can't ignore power and hope that it will go away and you can't claim that power isn't essential for your professional success. The issue for Black professional women isn't the *fact* of power; the issue is the relationship you choose to have with power.

You need to become comfortable with power. If you don't, you run the risk of losing control of your career path. But if you decide to acknowledge your power, it can help you. Ultimately, your embrace of power will position you to help others successfully shape their careers. Bringing along others once you have succeeded is especially important for Black women.

The key to having a successful relationship with power is acknowledging and overcoming the negative aspects and working to ensure that the positive aspects work for you rather than against you. Making it work is more than being OK with power, it's about embracing it, and this can be challenging. All worthwhile relationships involve hard work and commitment and your relationship with power is no different. It starts with you.

When a Decision about Your Career Is Not Up to You

There will be times when a decision about your career is not yours to make. In any challenging situation, the key factor is how you choose to respond. Even though the executive who bullied me early in my career once used this piece of advice as a verbal weapon, he was right. Choosing how to respond was the skill that carried me through the most important decision of my twenty-year career.

I was working late one evening and had popped out to my car to get my umbrella because rain had been predicted. It wasn't unusual for me to work late. I was the most productive in the evenings because my days were always filled with meetings. The peace of no interruptions gave me time to think and make decisions about my work, my leaders, and my team. I didn't realize that this evening was to be the most important thinking time I would ever experience.

When I returned from my car, I entered the front lobby and scanned my card to enter the building. My card didn't work the first time. I scanned it again and then a third time—it still didn't work.

The security guard and I both laughed; we thought I just probably needed a new one. I admitted to him that I had accidently washed my badge and card the week before and had let it dry out. That was the only reason I could think of as to why it didn't work. The security guard followed the standard protocol and picked up the phone to call his manager to obtain approval to let me into the building. I was happy to know that there were guards and practices in place to keep my workplace safe. I came to find out that I was now someone who didn't belong, who was to be kept out by these safeguards.

The security guard hung up the phone, turned to me, and said, "You are no longer employed." I was stunned. I didn't know how to respond. I didn't understand what was going on or what had just happened. I had come to work that day with the intent of returning the next morning, and every day thereafter.

The security guard told me to go home and call my manager. Fortunately the guard and I had a relationship. We knew each other. I asked him to call his superior again and ask him to give me permission to go back to my office so I could retrieve my personal items (purse, glasses, phones, etc.). In addition, the door to my office was open, confidential files were open on my desk, and I had left my computer on.

I was allowed back into my office with very strict instructions not to leave it at any time. I was told that if I needed to even go to the bathroom, I was to call security to escort me. I felt less than human. The words that the security guard said to me were words that I should have heard from a manager behind closed doors. Instead, I heard them from a security guard as we stood at a desk in a public space.

I went back to my office and followed the strict instructions that had been given to me. I pulled out a note that one of my leaders had handwritten to me as inspiration. It was in a folder labeled "Francine's Acknowledgments" that I had started very early in my career. I had carried it with me to each company where I had worked. I pulled it out on bad days to reaffirm my success.

This particular note stated:

> *Dear Francine,*
>
> *Just a brief note of thanks and support for your leadership. You are in a big role for us and I want you to know that you have my confidence to deliver on behalf of the company. Please let me know what you need to continue your success. I look forward to our partnership.*
>
> *Sam*

What I later found out was that Sam was the person behind the approval of my dismissal—the ultimate mastermind.

While this experience had certainly taken me by surprise in the moment, I knew what had precipitated it. For the few months preceding this event, I had been navigating a contentious, acrimonious, and challenging situation. It was one that went to the core of my value system, and my employer had asked something of me that went against everything I stood for, against the values I held most dear. I had refused to agree to do what they asked, and even demanded, that I do. The people I was speaking for did not have the power to speak for themselves. Because I had used my voice on their behalf, I became the one who was to be silenced.

I knew the potential consequences of my actions. I knew that not doing what the company was asking might mean giving up all that I had worked for, but I also knew what I believed was right. The many conversations I had heard in my house growing up and the stories my mother and father told me imparted the values that guided my every action. One of my values that I prized above all others was standing up and speaking up for those less fortunate than me. This was one of the times to stand up.

And as this incident made very clear, the company's position was that if I couldn't see it their way, then I no longer belonged there. But despite the risks, and even though I had hoped to carry my career forward at this company for many years yet, I simply could not agree with their position. Nothing—not a job, not my security, not the position I had worked so hard to achieve—was worth sacrificing what I stand for as a person. People have often told me that I live a very principled professional life. I always respond that that is how I live my life overall, not just at work.

Of course, this was a horrible way to find out I was no longer employed. Even my immediate manager didn't have the courage to speak to me directly. Unfortunately, we know of many instances where leaders are still informing employees about employment decisions by using technology—a poor choice.

As I sat there in my office, reflecting on my career and all that I had contributed, I came to the conclusion that I needed to do more. My career was far from over and I deserved more.

This was my power—the power to make decisions for myself and advocate on my own behalf. Then it dawned on me—I would go back to my original career plan. I had actually made a template of sorts. Nothing had changed and following this plan had always paid off for me. It had been with me since my very first promotion and I looked at it each year. It reaffirmed that I was on the right path and was doing the right things to build and create my success. This job may have been over, but I had everything that I had built for myself. I had my professional network and my power circle. I had my experience and a proven track record of success going back two decades. It was time to move forward, and I still had the tools and leverage to create something great for myself. No company, especially not one that would treat an employee like this and that would ask of me what they had asked, was going to get in the way of my career, my goals, or my life.

Your Principles Will Always Guide You

Your power is your voice. With your voice comes a responsibility to keep your word. I learned that when you are stripped down to the essence of who you are, the only thing that you have is your word. This is especially true in the workplace because being in the corporate environment always involves playing a competitive game, no matter what your race or gender or identity is. Remember that the corporate game has no rules, and even if you watch the players carefully, the people you trust will sometimes surprise you. They can and will change.

But what never changes is your word—you control that and you own that. I had given my word to people whose voices were not heard or acknowledged. I lent them my power and my voice because this was not about me. This was about navigating the system together.

There will be moments in your career when you will have to take a position and it will be hard to stand up to the system—a system which is inevitably controlled by the individuals who already possess enormous power. During such times, it might be easier to just sympathize with people who have less power than you do and walk away without taking action. But if you are a good leader or if you aspire to be one or if it is clear that you stand for something, you will have to make a decision. Your principles will be the only thing to guide you in such moments. These will be times when only you can decide what to do—and the decision will probably be a tough one.

In making the choice to support this group, I knew the company might end a job and position that I would have liked to continue. My decision was to give up a career in order to protect what I believed and stood for. This was a career that took care of me and my family. I had worked very hard for it and deserved it, but this time the situation wasn't about that. It was about what I stood for. My soul was not for sale.

Even though I was at the pinnacle of my career, this experience was another lesson for me. I learned that all things were not equal and that not everything is fair even after you've gotten that seat at the table. You have to ensure that you own your plan and that you have made alliances with others who can help you make your plan a reality. Your professional success is about being intentional and being focused on the future. Never let anyone or anything get in your way. The moment you do that, you have lost your power. And you have worked too hard to let that happen.

The Secret
to Your
Own
Power

Black women have never been known to be silent about what and who we believe in. This is evident in our actions in the realms of social justice, economic parity, and politics, to name just a few examples. However, in the workplace, where we spend most of our time, we are often silent. This is the place where many of us give 100 percent and make tremendous sacrifices. The workplace does not meet our expectations and it continues to fail us.

I am a firm believer that you have to be in the room to change the room, and there is a huge need for change in a lot of the rooms in the institutions where Black professional women work. This is the case regardless of which room you are in or what table you are sitting at, whether it is the big table or just the conference room where you are taking notes in your first job. Making change comes down to using one of the most powerful tools that you have—your voice.

It is so important to be declarative about what you want from your career. You need to make sure that your organization can support your professional goals. For example, if your goal is to lead a business unit and having a profit and loss responsibility is required (as in most companies), tell your managers and other leaders that that is what you want. Make sure the roles you are offered include opportunities that will lead to your goal and that you are transparent about those goals. Transparency ensures that you and your employer share the same expectations.

Yes, you want people to speak on your behalf, to be able to speak about you when you are not in the room, to stand up and speak for you even when you don't know that you are being attacked or scrutinized. But it starts with you using your voice to position them so they can position you.

This is the only way that you will hold the organization, its leadership, your manager—anyone who is a supporter of your career—accountable. Tell them often what you expect. Hold them accountable as much as they hold you accountable to deliver business results for your organization. You may not know all the ins and outs of your organization or who the power players are or even how to play your best power hand, but your voice allows you to ask. Ask about all the things that you do not know and want to master. At a minimum, you will receive a basic answer. And you may receive much more than that, a detailed analysis of a situation that gives you information you need to make strategic decisions and position yourself for success.

You may tire of asking and your voice may become hoarse, but you can't stop. When you stop using your voice, you've given up your true power. When others have all the power to talk about you and your career, you may not like what they have to say. No matter what level you have reached in your organization, who you report to, what your role is, or what rooms you are in or not in, your voice is the power can use to move yourself forward.

What I Want for You

The intention of this book is to prepare you to ask for the right things to get you to the next level in your career. I've talked about understanding power and how to use it to your advantage for things such as sponsorship, advocacy throughout an organization, and building the right professional network. I've shared my experiences to show you how you can play your best power hand even in tough situations. I hope I've helped you understand how power works in your organization, which person or persons have it, what they value, and how to build the relationships that will be to your advantage. Remember, those relationships are about a reciprocal exchange: you have something people in power want and they have something you want. In my case, I wanted access to powerful people and success in my career and the people in power I sought out often wanted to know what I knew and what my thoughts were. The relationships I built from this exchange ultimately became my power.

The most important thing I did was to ensure that I never lost my voice. Sometimes what I had to say paid off and sometimes it didn't. Some of my actions were guarded and some were risky. But I used my ability to speak up about myself and for folks who looked like me.

A recent report on women in the workplace by LeanIn and McKinsey & Company included a fact that I already knew to be true. *Women in the Workplace 2019* said that as many Black women as white men who were surveyed (41 percent for both groups) wanted to become executives. We have already demonstrated our desire to succeed, our self-efficacy, our belief in our self-worth, and our steadfast pursuit of what we want and professionally.

The issue when Black women enter the workplace is that we don't always know the path to success. We aren't given a road map, much less any indication that we are heading in the right direction. Sometimes we don't speak up until it's too late. That lateness only compounds our frustration and our weariness about seeing others promoted. When we ask why we have been overlooked, we often don't receive an honest answer.

I believe that leveraging your voice strategically is the only way to change the institutions we work in. Yes, it is hard to get in the room. It is even harder to obtain a seat at the table where your voice counts and to then keep that seat. The path to that seat begins with the conversations that you must initiate with your organization and its leaders.

Ask questions of your supervisors and leaders. Let them know your expectations about where your career is going and who in your organization is helping you get there. Use your voice to say, "This is where I want to be, so how do I get there?"

Please don't believe the myth that you alone own your career. Everyone needs the support of others to succeed. I've never seen anyone accomplish anything truly meaningful on their own in the companies I've worked for. Your organization is no different, no matter how big or how small it is.

You have to use your voice to hold those in your organization accountable no matter your level. Your organization has an expectation that you give them 100 percent of yourself as an employee, so why would you let them, in return, give you anything less. Getting what you want and what you deserve in your career should be an expectation you have of your workplace, because your organization has that expectation of you. They have told you that they are committed to your success. No employer will ever say anything less.

But we're committed to our success as well as Black women. We're both on the same page and aligned on that piece. We're all saying the same thing.

How Far We've Come and How Far We Have Left to Go

Many of us have been striving for this success for a very long time. Organizations have been saying that they support our success for a long time. I heard this when I began my career back when the data labeled me an African American female. My mother tells me stories from the time when she heard herself labeled as a Negro. The bias that exists in our world is not as pointed and pronounced as it was then, but it is also accurate to say that many things still have not changed. We still have a long way to go and we are not there just yet.

Black women know that we are still not in enough positions of leadership and authority. This is why it is so imperative that you use your voice to advocate for yourself. You must speak up for yourself and ask why or why not. If you are not getting the professional career opportunities you want, why aren't you, and what can you do about it? I implore you to look around and use your voice to ask for what you want. Make your intentions known, be strategic, and use the skills you've learned here in this book.

So if you are pressed for time and have chosen to read only this chapter, here are three things to remember about the importance of your voice.

1. Your work is about power and managing it, not just about having a seat at the table. Learn how leaders in your organization use power. Black women in corporate America are still playing a game that we were not trained for that operates with a set of rules that were not designed with us in mind. We are also assessed on our command of a set of skills that probably don't appear in your company's leadership guide. You'll need to listen and watch carefully to learn what the unwritten rules of your organization are. Also pay close attention to how the leaders and C-suite executives in your company use their power. What do they do that identifies them as leaders in your organization? Do they have a unique brand? What are they known for in your organization? Who knows them? What does their network look like? Who are their sponsors?

2. Use the qualities and behaviors you observe as a road map to power. Learn the subtextual skills leaders exhibit that have made them successful at your company. Pay attention to what the company rewards them for.

3. Establish your own power circle, a group of trusted advisors that can provide you with valuable information and help you. These should be people who understand what your organization values—the people, the roles, the functions, the initiatives, and the important information that will help you navigate through the company and ensure that you are positioned to succeed. Your network should

consist of individuals who will always watch out for you and who have your best interest in mind.

4. Once you have joined the ranks of people in power, don't be lulled into a false sense of security. Nothing is permanent except the fact that you are Black. Remember that you are only as valuable as your last amazing project or the most recent time you saved your company millions of dollars. You can't ever rely only on your past successes. The work you will do to remain at the table is important not just for you but also for other women and especially the other women of color who are in the room with you and those who are still working to get into the room. Your network will become increasingly important as you excel in your career.

5. Remember that you always need to offer your allies something in return for the help they give you. Know what your currency is in your company and what it is worth.

6. You don't have to be like everyone else, but you do have to understand what it takes to get there. The higher up you go, the more you represent your organization. Sometimes your individuality and even who you are will take a backseat.

7. Include people outside your company in your network. The network that you worked so hard to create may disappear in your organization. If your sponsor leaves the company, the people they sponsored may go too. This is why it is important to have an internal and external professional network.

8. As a Black woman, you will often be called upon to balance multiple roles in your job, your career, and your family. You may be forced to make some choices between these three things at times. I had to make such choices sometimes and I didn't always make the best decisions. When your company is asking too much at the expense of time with your family, the decision is in your hands whether you will leave or stay. The key is to be well aware of what you are staying with or stepping away from.

9. Always know what you are and are not willing to do. If you don't stand for something, you won't stand for anything. Getting a seat at your organization's leadership table does require a certain amount of risk-taking. Know what you are walking into. Know the price of having a seat at the leadership table and always be prepared to step away.

10. Most important, remember the voice you have and the power you already have as a Black professional woman. Use your power strategically to advance your career.

The power game has no rules, so make sure you play by the rules that are of value to you and that you believe in. When all is said and done, the only person you need be accountable to is you. Be powerful enough to own your voice and build the career and life that you choose!

The Leader's Role in Helping Black Women

My Message to Corporate Leaders

Leadership and power go hand in hand.

Most important, this work is the responsibility of leadership, not a grassroots activity, as many leaders and organizations have thus far assumed. The burden of change, and I do mean burden, is too often placed on the woman, especially the Black woman, and she is often the one with the lesser power. I would be remiss if I did not look at the role leaders have to play in advancing Black professional women in the workplace.

There is a tendency toward aggregating data, which erases whether we are speaking of women, women of color, or Black women. This erases the distinctions between groups, and as a result, the same thinking is applied to all of us when this should not be the case. This causes us to miss recognizing true opportunities to make the most significant impact. In the corporate world, if you focus your efforts on the biggest opportunity, you can make the biggest impact. The biggest opportunity to promote women in the workplace is with Black professional women. Black women are the least represented group in leadership and C-suite positions in the corporate sector.

You have all the data you need and if you choose to look further, there are a myriad of groups where you can find the research; hear the stories of women of color and Black women who come to work every day—these women work for you. If you hire a consultant, hire them to help you truly understand *how* to fix your problem concerning the lack of Black women in leadership. To solve this problem will demand more than general recommendations and discussion. Hire them from end to end, and engage them to help you implement their solutions, not just give you advice. Let them help you to be accountable and hold them accountable as well.

Start by Looking Within

If you must see the data and validate it, do what I call the Org. Chart Test. Take a close, comprehensive look at your organizational charts. Make sure to segment and look specifically at the management teams, E-suite and C-suite, and even your Board of Directors.

As you look at this data, ask: where are the Black women within your organization? At what levels? What jobs do they hold? What are the true paths to such leadership positions? Are the Black women in your organization on those paths?

Most important, do you know any of the Black women in your organization? How do you know them? Taking time to do this is work is the true data and should be all that you need in order to make an impact.

This data should provide enough information for you to recognize the gravity of the situation. The answers are often not what we feel they should be, so we deflect and avoid. And if that will hold you back, just don't get caught up in data that will handicap you. It is far more important to simply start taking action.

The purpose and intention of this book is to share with Black women how to play, and ultimately master, the power game. As a leader, you play the power game every day. You set the rules. In reality, there are no true rules, just the ones that leadership makes and that people choose to follow. As a global executive once myself, I know that it is you who sets the tone and provides the leadership. That is what I did as well. You, as the leader, have the power to make change. The question is: what do you choose to do with this power? How will you use it to make the change necessary to help Black women succeed in their careers?

Recognize Your Own Power

Hopefully many readers of this book are people who can make the decisions and take the actions to drive the change we need. If you are in that group, you have the power to help Black women succeed in your workplace. Change starts at the leadership level, not the other way around, in my experience. You can start by simply telling Black women what is important to you and what is important to the organization. We understand that the rules change all the time because the world of business is very dynamic. Help the Black women you lead learn the unwritten rules and the skills that no one talks about. This is the power game Black women need to understand so they can play their best hand.

Take a step back and access your career path and what got you to where you are today. It wasn't luck. You weren't just in the right place at the right time. I have often heard this from leaders, which is unfortunate as it misses the sponsors, hard work, and relationships that got them to the positions they hold. Think about how you can help Black women in your organization access those same resources.

Match the Black women in your company with the right sponsors and help them navigate within your organization, master their professional story, and build a network that will work for them both in public and behind the scenes. Ensure that they have access to leaders and initiatives that will position them for their next promotion. Work with them to ensure that their development plan is robust and relates to the business outcomes your company is focused on.

I recognize that this is not easy. It is hard work. It is uncomfortable. But you have the opportunity to share and provide access to and most importantly, commit to this journey. Think about how uncomfortable Black women may be when they meet you and realize that you have nothing in common. The goal is to get past that and it will take some time. But it begins with you as a leader.

Women in corporate America are often told that they need to own their careers. Black women have been owning whatever they have been given for decades. We know that we have the ability to do amazing things.

Actions You Can Take to Help Black Professional Women

Here are a few actions you can take to go beyond the words and the goodwill corporations like to present to the world at large. We need more than the slogans and images your corporate communications team produces about how your company supports Black women's advancement. We need actions that will have a lasting impact.

1. **As soon as possible, help the Black women you hire learn how to navigate within your company's power structure.**

    Often it will be the case that the people with power in your company won't have experiences in common with Black women. *That is OK.* You can form relationships with Black women that will benefit your company by telling them about the qualities and behaviors your company values. Make it a point to ensure that support structures are set up to help Black women succeed early in their careers. See that Black women have mentors who are committed to helping them avoid things that would derail their careers.

2. **Make it a priority to hire Black women leaders.**

    Look at Black women as future leaders. If they are already members of your organization at lower levels on your organization chart, work with them to prepare them for leadership and then make sure that they get promoted into leadership positions. Remove the barriers to promotion to a management position, that first step toward a career as a leader. If your organization hasn't hired enough Black professional women to make substantial and lasting change in your organizational chart, find them in the marketplace. Hold your peers accountable to do this as well. Talk with them to give them insight that can help your company achieve robust representation of Black women at the highest levels of leadership.

3. **Help Black women succeed after they are promoted to leadership positions.**

Promotion to a new role or position within an organization does not guarantee continued success. It is just the starting point. Continue to watch the careers of Black women who are promoted in your company. Make sure that they continue to have the sponsors and support they need to succeed as they move up. Share the unwritten rules about how people in power operate in your organization. Tell them important things about your company's culture. Institute policies that will help Black women balance doing their jobs, managing their careers, and caring for their families.

4. **Use your power to remove institutional barriers.**

Remove the institutional barriers, both apparent and not apparent, that you own or have accountability for. These are the barriers in your organization's infrastructure, systems, routines, and policies and procedures that may force a Black woman to leave the company or to prevent her from succeeding even though she is as capable as other members of the "power club." Support Black women in leadership in the same way you support the leaders who look like you.

If you see something happening that may serve as a road-block to a Black woman's success within your organization, work on removing the roadblock so that she doesn't have to make a decision to leave her job over a battle she knows she can't win. If you don't know what those battles look like, take the time to ask Black women in your company what they are. A person's perception is their reality, so don't dismiss or ignore the issues they tell you about. Once you dig into perception, it often reveals itself as truth. Please get to those true truths.

Let's all focus on evening out the playing field. Women, especially Black women, aren't usually given access to information about how to successfully advance their careers. I've given Black women the tools to open dialogues with you so they can work with you to position themselves for leadership roles. You have the power to do something significant about advancing Black professional women in your workplace. They'll be knocking on your office door if they've taken my advice to heart. Be ready to work with them to increase their access to power.

Please
Sit
Over
There

As helpful as the information in this book is intended to be, it is your independent thinking and the discussions I hope the book will provoke that will be the real drivers of change. This discussion guide will help you think about and discuss strategies and tactics that will enable your professional success and advancement. You can answer the questions on your own or with a reading group, solidarity group, an employee or business resource group, or with your colleagues at work.

These questions are also a great way to engage with your managers and other members of your leadership team. They will provide opportunities for you to exchange perspectives, thoughts, and opinions that may lead to stronger professional relationships. Nothing is stronger than having the support of like-minded individuals who are focused on helping you with your professional success.

General Questions

1. What new things have you learned about from the book?

2. What questions do you have about what you learned?

3. What did you see as the central strategy the book recommends? How can you apply it to your career? To your workplace? To working with your leaders?

4. What points in the book resonated with you?

Charting Your Career Path

1. What are your career goals? What do you want out of life? Think big!

2. Think about your answer to question 1 and where you are in your career right now. What would a path from where you are now to where you want to be look like?

Identifying Power in Your Organization and Field

1. What are the informal structures of power in your organization? The formal power structure should be obvious from the hierarchical organizational chart. But do people in the higher levels of power on that chart really have the most power?

   a. Who in your organization gets their proposals consistently approved?

   b. Whose judgment is consistently considered to be sound?

   c. Who is known in your organization for their leadership and how do they work with their team and others?

   d. Who has a reputation for positioning others to succeed?

2. Which of the people you have identified can you reach out to and attempt to begin a relationship with? Think about the types of connections you might have with the people you've identified. It might be that your job responsibilities contribute to the projects they lead. Perhaps you went to the same school. Maybe someone on your list has the kind of role or job that you are aiming for. Make a list of at least five people to start with.

3. Commit that you will all reach out to each of these five people. Next time your group meets, discuss how your attempts to build relationships are going, including whether you are getting responses, how to prepare for the meetings you were able to schedule, how any meetings you had went, and what you are doing to follow up. (Remember not to consider a lack of response a no. Try again after an appropriate interval; these are very busy people!)

4. Do your research on each person who agrees to meet with you. Find out what school they went to, what their career trajectory has been, what specific things they've achieved, what connections you share, what their values are (which you can intuit from the groups they volunteer for, for example), and so forth. Then brainstorm about the questions you can ask them about how they got to where they are. What about their experiences intrigues you? What are you hoping to learn from each person? Make your questions very specific to each person you are able to meet with.

Your Professional Network

1. Do an assessment of your professional network. Who do you know? What is your relationship to each person in your network? Consider people in your organization, people who work for another organization in your field, and people outside your immediate field who have positions that would be of interest to you.

2. Does your network include the power players you identified in the previous exercise? If not, how can you start building a network that includes those people?

3. What do you do on a regular basis to maintain your relationships with the people in your network? What can you start doing that would grow and strengthen your relationships with people in the network you want to have?

4. Remember relationships in your network go both ways. What can you offer the people you are forming connections with? Always start a connection or a relationship by discerning what you have that they value. A good question to ask in any meeting is "How can I help you?"

Sponsorship

1. What new information did you learn from this book about how sponsorship works? How will those new criteria inform your search for sponsors?

2. Consider the career goals you have identified for yourself. What positions or skills would be valuable to you in your next sponsor? Who in your organization do you have a connection with that is well placed to support the next step you have identified for your career?

3. If you have a sponsor, what traits have made that person a good sponsor for you?

4. What things do you feel you should be mindful of as you are trying to prepare to develop a relationship with a sponsor?

To Leave or to Stay

1. Have you ever had to leave a job because it wasn't the right fit? Have you ever had to leave a job because it required you to make compromises that violated your values? Have you ever had to leave a job because you weren't getting the opportunities you wanted? There is power in sharing our experiences—discuss in your group who has done this and why.

2. Assess your current role in terms of whether it offers you what you will need to advance in your career and reach your goals. Do you have the right connections to take you there? If you don't, do you see the potential for building those connections?

3. If your assessment in the previous question makes you think you may not be able to achieve your goals with your current employer, move on to considering your extended network. Who outside your organization has a role like the next role you would like to achieve? Who supports your work and your career?

4. Reach out to at least five people outside your organization and request meetings, and revisit your progress regularly with the group.

Being a Black Professional Woman

1. What are the biggest obstacles you face in your organization as a Black woman? How do you think you might be able to overcome them? How can you enlist the help of others as you work to overcome these barriers to your success?

2. Have you experienced exclusion at work? How have you responded to being excluded? How have your responses impacted your career? Did you take actions designed to ensure that you were included in your organization?

3. What does true allyship in action look like for you? How do you determine if allyship is genuine?

4. How have you challenged yourself to speak up even in the face of adversity?

5. What work experiences do you think your white colleagues need to know about? What strategies can you use to make sure that white colleagues are more aware of these experiences?

Acknowledgments

It's all about the relationships!

From the relationships that I developed many decades ago to the ones I forged last week, I am truly grateful for every individual. I believe that we all have something important to say; that our voices and messages matter, regardless as to who you are or where you come from.

The journey to writing this book started a long time ago when I fell in love with the power of the written word. My mother, Juanita Dickey Parham, and my father, Oscar Parham Sr., filled our home with books and encouraged me to read everything I could get my hands on. They also taught me the power of meaningful conversation. I was surrounded by ideas and a team of idealists—my five siblings, Oscar Parham Jr., Nikki Parham, Lisa Parham-Grady, Maria Parham, and Mark Parham. As I grew up, their perspectives and thinking helped shape me. You supported and encouraged me in anything I did. My parents also served as role models as I raised my son, Christopher Parham-Darabi. The little boy that I once cheered on, telling him that he could achieve anything he wanted to do, now cheers me on as an adult and plays back that same message to me.

Writing a book has always been an aspiration for me, but it had always been something I would get to eventually, some time in the future. It wasn't until I was introduced to an amazing Latina woman, Denise Padin-Collazom, the author of *Thriving in the Fight: A Survival Manual for Latinas on the Front Lines of Change*, that I was inspired to write my story. Denise challenged me to amplify my voice and introduced me to her publisher, Berrett-Koehler, and its founder, Steve Piersanti.

Steve brought in Anna Leinberger, who served not only as my editor extraordinaire, thought partner, and coach as I wrote this book but also as someone who cared deeply about what I had to say as a Black woman in this world. As it's said, we all have a book inside us. But the real task is having the fortitude to get the book out, to share our thoughts on paper, and to send them into the world for others to experience. Anna helped me to do exactly this, helping me to get all my thoughts, experiences, and the stories of two decades into this book—an amazing feat! And the day Valerie Brewster Caldwell, Associate Director of Design and Production, officially announced the front cover of my book designed by Nita Ybarra, I knew my work had truly become a reality. Jeevan Sivasubramaniam, the Managing Director, Editorial, and Courtney Schonfeld, Senior Manager, Production and Audio, took it from there, as did many other Berrett-Koehler team members behind-the-scenes. I am deeply grateful for their expertise and their support for my book.

I have so many to thank for being with me on my journey through life. I am deeply grateful to my friends and to amazing colleagues who have become friends. That list includes Shamita Alwani-Kumar, Pavan Bhatia, Kailei Carr, Joyel Crawford, Christopher Etienne, Adam Grant, Minda Harts, Karen Jaw-Madson, Cassandra Johnson, Lisa Kaplowitz, Bev Kaye, Vonda Page, Aparna Ramaswamy, Christine Robinson, Laura Sabattini, Renee Selman, Michael Shapiro, Michelle Snow, Carlett Spike, Felicia Stephenson, and Jessica Valentin. Each of you always picked up the phone, read my emails and text messages, checked on me, and supported me and my sometimes half-baked ideas. Most important, you cared for me both when things were going well for me and when I was facing challenges. I know that I can always depend on each of you, just as you can depend on me. That's our bond.

This book would not have been possible without the sage advice of the first readers of my manuscript. Thank you, Shabnam Banerjee-McFarland, Terri Frick, and Elizabeth McKellar. Your feedback was invaluable and gave me a more robust framework to work with.

Most important, I thank God from whom all blessings flow. I am truly blessed to receive.

I now have even more to say, so stay tuned for the next book! I'll be counting on each of you again. My voice is powerful and I have even more to say about helping women and women of color advance in the workplace.

Onward and always upward!

Index

About Francine Parham

Francine Parham is a career expert who focuses on female leadership and preparing women and women of color advance to positions of leadership and authority in the workplace. She brings her two decades of experience in the corporate sector to the work that she and her organization do.

Francine speaks about topics such as navigating the workplace and holding leadership accountable to help women and women of color advance professionally. She is the coauthor of *The Ultimate Career Pocket Guide* and is a contributing author to the Columbia Journalism School's *The Memory Project*. She has been recognized as a career expert by the Women's Media

Center. She is a Senior Fellow at the Conference Board, a member-driven global think tank in which she also serves as a Steering Committee Member of the Human Capital Center for their Diversity, Equity and Inclusion Institute and their Total Rewards Institute.

Francine holds two master's degrees, earning a Master of Science in journalism from Columbia University as a Stabile Investigative Fellow and a Master of Arts in labor and industrial relations from the University of Illinois. Her undergraduate degree is from Purdue University, where she majored in business communications and psychology. She is the proud mother of a son who works with her to advance women and women of color in the workplace.

About Francine Parham & Co.

Francine has been one of the few Black women to reach the executive level, having held the position of global vice-president in two Fortune 500 companies: General Electric and Johnson and Johnson. She understands the importance of having the right skills that are often implicit and opaque within organizations to achieve professional success as a woman or woman of color in the workplace. Inspired to help women and women of color master and utilize such skills for their professional advancement, she founded FrancineParham & Co.

FrancineParham & Co. is a professional development company focused on helping organizations prepare and position their female talent with career advancement skills, strategies, and approaches they need for their success. Francine is the creator of the Sharpen Your Skills Professional™, a series of career development learning programs focused on the right skills (explicit and implicit) women and women of color need for their professional success and advancement at work. Her company also works with organizations to provide quantitative and qualitative assessments with recommended approaches and solutions to advance their professional women and women of color in the workplace.

Berrett–Koehler
Publishers

Berrett-Koehler is an independent publisher dedicated to an ambitious mission: *Connecting people and ideas to create a world that works for all.*

Our publications span many formats, including print, digital, audio, and video. We also offer online resources, training, and gatherings. And we will continue expanding our products and services to advance our mission.

We believe that the solutions to the world's problems will come from all of us, working at all levels: in our society, in our organizations, and in our own lives. Our publications and resources offer pathways to creating a more just, equitable, and sustainable society. They help people make their organizations more humane, democratic, diverse, and effective (and we don't think there's any contradiction there). And they guide people in creating positive change in their own lives and aligning their personal practices with their aspirations for a better world.

And we strive to practice what we preach through what we call "The BK Way." At the core of this approach is *stewardship,* a deep sense of responsibility to administer the company for the benefit of all of our stakeholder groups, including authors, customers, employees, investors, service providers, sales partners, and the communities and environment around us. Everything we do is built around stewardship and our other core values of *quality, partnership, inclusion,* and *sustainability.*

This is why Berrett-Koehler is the first book publishing company to be both a B Corporation (a rigorous certification) and a benefit corporation (a for-profit legal status), which together require us to adhere to the highest standards for corporate, social, and environmental performance. And it is why we have instituted many pioneering practices (which you can learn about at www.bkconnection.com), including the Berrett-Koehler Constitution, the Bill of Rights and Responsibilities for BK Authors, and our unique Author Days.

We are grateful to our readers, authors, and other friends who are supporting our mission. We ask you to share with us examples of how BK publications and resources are making a difference in your lives, organizations, and communities at www.bkconnection.com/impact.

Dear reader,

Thank you for picking up this book and welcome to the worldwide BK community! You're joining a special group of people who have come together to create positive change in their lives, organizations, and communities.

What's BK all about?

Our mission is to connect people and ideas to create a world that works for all.

Why? Our communities, organizations, and lives get bogged down by old paradigms of self-interest, exclusion, hierarchy, and privilege. But we believe that can change. That's why we seek the leading experts on these challenges—and share their actionable ideas with you.

A welcome gift

To help you get started, we'd like to offer you a **free copy** of one of our bestselling ebooks:

www.bkconnection.com/welcome

When you claim your **free ebook**, you'll also be subscribed to our blog.

Our freshest insights

Access the best new tools and ideas for leaders at all levels on our blog at ideas.bkconnection.com.

Sincerely,

Your friends at Berrett-Koehler

Certified

Corporation